Bet Smart:
The Kelly System for Gambling and Investing

Stefan Hollos and Richard Hollos
QuantWolf.com
Exstrom Laboratories LLC
Longmont, Colorado

Abrazol Publishing

an imprint of Exstrom Laboratories LLC
662 Nelson Park Drive, Longmont, CO 80503-7674 U.S.A.

Publisher's Cataloging in Publication Data

Hollos, Stefan
Bet Smart: The Kelly System for Gambling and Investing
/ by Stefan Hollos and Richard Hollos
p. cm.
Includes bibliographical references and index.
ISBN 978-1-887187-01-5
Library of Congress Control Number: 2008909828
1. Games of chance (Mathematics). 2. Gambling–Mathematical models.
I. Title. II. Hollos, Stefan.
QA271.H3 2008
519.2 HOL

Contents

Dedicated to our parents, Istvan and Anna Hollos, for their faith in us.

Preface

This book is about gambling systems with a particular emphasis on the Kelly system. A gambling system is a method for choosing bet sizes in order to maximize winnings and minimize the potential for loss. A good gambling system is a systematic method for managing money and risk.

Now you may ask if such a thing is even possible. Are there really money management methods that will increase your winnings? The answer for most gambling situations is no. The reason is that most of the gambling games that you will encounter in a casino for example, have what is called negative expectation. This means that in the long run you are almost always guaranteed to lose money playing these games. There is no gambling system that can make a negative expectation, or for that matter a zero expectation, game profitable.

A gambling system is only useful when confronted with a positive expectation game and such games are rare. The simplest example of a positive expectation gambling game is the simple coin toss bet with a biased coin. This is a coin where one of the sides, heads say, comes up more often than the other. If heads has a probability greater than 0.5 of coming up and you are able to bet on it repeatedly, then you will make money in the long run. In this case a gambling system can help you increase your winnings.

Probably the place where you are most likely to find a positive expectation gamble is in the financial markets. People do not usually associate investing with gambling but there really is no fundamental difference. Every investment is a gamble with the potential for losing or gaining money. If you had to draw a distinction between a gamble and an investment it would be that an investment usually has a small probability of total loss. This is one of the reasons why there are so many more positive expectation investments than gambling games.

Most of the gambling systems developed by gamblers base bet sizes on the size of previous bets and whether those bets were won or lost. These systems tend to produce large fluctuations in bankroll, both up and down. Since these systems do not take bankroll size into account when selecting a bet size, the chance of going bankrupt with such a system is high. The most common example of such a system is the Martingale system which is analyzed in chapter 2.

The Kelly system takes bankroll size into account by always betting a fixed fraction of the size of the bankroll. The fraction is selected so that the bankroll grows exponentially at the fastest possible rate in the long run. It is important to note that exponential growth only happens in the long run with the Kelly system. Considerable short term fluctuations are still possible with the Kelly system but since the amount wagered is based on the size of the bankroll, the probability of going bust is small. The Kelly system is discussed in detail in chapters 3 and 4.

In order to analyze gambling systems in detail, a significant amount of mathematics must be used. The treatment of gambling systems in this book is therefore highly mathematical. To get the most out of this book you should have a good familiarity with mathematical notation and have taken at least one calculus course. It would also be very helpful to have had some exposure to probability theory. The essential concepts from probability theory are reviewed in chapter 1 but to really understand the presentation it will help to have had a previous course in the subject.

Following the probability theory review in chapter 1, chapter 2 looks at some of the more commonly used gambling systems. Multiple bet state systems are analyzed as well as the Martingale and a simple cancellation system. For all these systems, the expectation and variance of the bankroll in a simple coin toss gambling game is calculated. For some systems it is not possible, or it is too complicated, to express the expectation and variance in a closed mathematical form. In this case Python code for performing the calculation is given.

Chapter 3 begins the analysis of the Kelly system. It starts with an analysis of fixed fraction betting in general. The question of how one chooses the fraction is considered next. Two approaches to answering this question are examined. One approach is to use the concept of a utility function which was first proposed by Daniel Bernoulli in 1738. The second approach is the one used by John Kelly. Kelly's approach is to choose the fraction so as to maximize the long term exponential growth rate of the bankroll. A discussion of Kelly's analogy between this growth rate and the rate of information transmission through a communications channel is included. Both the Kelly and Bernoulli approach lead to the conclusion that the optimal betting fraction is the one that maximizes the expectation of the logarithm of the bankroll. The rest of the chapter examines the calculation of the betting fraction, the expectation and variance of the bankroll, and the bankroll probabilities for single and multiple games. The chapter ends with a somewhat unusual application of the Kelly system to playing the Powerball Lottery.

The final chapter looks at the use of the Kelly system in investing. It starts out by looking at a single stock investment. This is more complicated than most gambling games since a stock investment can have many possible returns. Solving for the Kelly fraction in this case usually involves using numerical techniques. This is discussed in the text, and Python code for calculating the fraction is included. The calculation of the Kelly fraction when there is the possibility of including a risk free bond with the stock is taken up next. An interesting application of this is calculating the default probabilities of risky bonds based simply on their market interest rates. The chapter concludes by looking at the calculation of the Kelly fraction for investing in two stocks simultaneously. This must also be done numerically and Python code for the calculation is included.

This book is by no means an exhaustive treatment of the Kelly system but it should serve as a good introduction to the subject and a starting point for further investigation. Those wishing to delve further into the subject can consult the references at the end of the book.

This book has a website, where software and related information can be found:

`http://quantwolf.com/betsmart.html`

We can be reached by email at:
stefan@exstrom.com   richard@exstrom.com

Stefan Hollos and Richard Hollos
QuantWolf.com
Exstrom Laboratories LLC
Longmont, Colorado
November 2008

First, some legwork.

Chapter 1

Mathematical Introduction

1.1 Random Variables

A random variable assigns a number to each possible outcome of a random event.

A coin toss is an example of a random event with two possible outcomes: heads or tails. A random variable for the coin toss could for example assign the number 1 to heads and the number 0 to tails. A series of coin tosses would then be represented by a series of 1's and 0's.

Another example of a random event is the roll of a dice. In this case the obvious choice of random variable would be the number of dots on the side of the dice facing up.

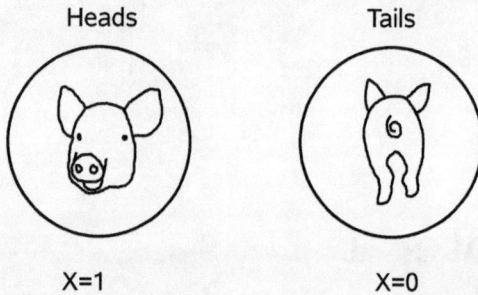

Figure 1.1: A random variable for the coin toss.

These are two examples of what are called discrete random variables.

A discrete random variable can have only a finite number of values or at most a countably infinite number of values which means that it has no more values than the set of natural numbers $1, 2, 3, \ldots$. A random variable may also be continuous. The weight of a person selected at random is an example of a continuous random variable.

1.2   Mean of a Random Variable

It is nice to be able to reduce all the values of a random variable to a single representative number. The three most common ones are

1. Mode - the value of a random variable that has the highest probability.

2. Median - a number chosen so that exactly half of the values of the random variable are below and half are above the number.

3. Mean - this is the average or probability weighted sum of the values of the random variable.

It is possible for all three of these numbers to be equal.

The mean is the most useful single number representation of a random variable and it is easy to derive a simple formula to calculate it. Let $x_i, i = 1, 2, \ldots m$ represent the possible values of a random variable. If N values of the random variable are generated, let $n_i, i = 1, 2, \ldots m$ represent the number of times that the value x_i occurs. The average of the N values is then

$$\sum_{i=1}^{m} \frac{n_i x_i}{N} \tag{1.1}$$

As N becomes very large, the ratio of n_i to N will become equal to the probability of x_i occurring as the value of the random variable. In the limit of infinitely large N, eq.1.1 becomes

$$\mu = \sum_{i=1}^{m} p(x_i) x_i \tag{1.2}$$

where $p(x_i)$ is the probability of x_i and μ is the commonly used symbol for the mean. The mean of a random vari-

able is also often called the expectation and eq.1.2 may be
expressed as

$$E[X] = \sum_{i=1}^{m} p(x_i)x_i \qquad (1.3)$$

where X is used to represent the random variable that can
take on the values x_i with probabilities $P(X = x_i) = p(x_i)$.

1.3 Properties of the Mean

It is sometimes necessary to calculate the sum or product
of random variables. For two random variables X and Y
with values $x_i, i = 1, 2, \ldots m$ and $y_j, j = 1, 2, \ldots n$ the mean
or expectation of their sum is

$$E[X + Y] = \sum_{i=1}^{m} \sum_{j=1}^{n} p(x_i, y_j)(x_i + y_j) \qquad (1.4)$$

where the function $p(x_i, y_j)$ is called the joint probability
distribution of X and Y. It is the probability that $X = x_i$ at the same time that $Y = y_j$. The joint probability
distribution has the following properties

$$\sum_{j=1}^{n} p(x_i, y_j) = p(x_i) \qquad (1.5)$$

$$\sum_{i=1}^{m} p(x_i, y_j) = p(y_j) \qquad (1.6)$$

These equations should be intuitively obvious. If for a given value of $X = x_i$, you sum the joint probabilities over all possible values of Y then you simply get the probability of x_i and vice versa. When X and Y are independent, meaning that $X = x_i$ has no effect on the probability that $Y = y_j$, then the joint probability can be written as the product of the individual probabilities

$$p(x_i, y_j) = p(x_i)p(y_j) \qquad (1.7)$$

An example of independent random variables is the numbers that show up on the roll of two dice. The value that shows up on one of the dice can in no way affect, or provide information about, the value that shows up on the other dice. In the case of fair dice, where all 6 values of the first dice, $X = 1, 2, 3, 4, 5, 6$ have the probability $p(x_i) = \frac{1}{6}$, and all 6 values of the second dice, $Y = 1, 2, 3, 4, 5, 6$, have the probability $p(y_j) = \frac{1}{6}$, the probability of any pair of values occurring is $p(x_i, y_j) = \frac{1}{6} \cdot \frac{1}{6} = \frac{1}{36}$.

When the two random variables are dependent then eq.1.7 does not hold. An example of dependent random variables is the roll of two dice – one red, one blue. Random variable 1 is the number on the red dice. Random variable 2 is the number that's the sum of the red and blue dice. Clearly in this case the value of the second random variable depends on the value of the first.

Using eq.'s 1.5 and 1.6 in eq.1.4 it is easy to show that

$$E[X + Y] = E[X] + E[Y] \qquad (1.8)$$

The expectation of the sum of two random variables is equal to the sum of their expectations. This is true whether the variables are dependent or independent.

Derivation of eq.1.8.
Eq.1.4 can first of all be written as

$$
\begin{aligned}
E[X + Y] &= \sum_i x_i \sum_j p(x_i, y_j) + \sum_j y_j \sum_i p(x_i, y_j) \\
&= \sum_i x_i p(x_i) + \sum_j y_j p(y_j) \\
&= E[X] + E[Y]
\end{aligned}
$$

Eq.1.8 can be extended to the sum of any finite number of random variables

$$E[X + Y + \ldots + Z] = E[X] + E[Y] + \ldots + E[Z] \quad (1.9)$$

One further extension is to the case where each random variable is multiplied by a constant. If X is multiplied by the constant a and Y is multiplied by the constant b then

$$E[aX + bY] = aE[X] + bE[Y] \qquad (1.10)$$

This is the linearity property of the expectation.

The expectation of the product of the random variable X and Y is

$$E[XY] = \sum_{i=1}^{m} \sum_{j=1}^{n} p(x_i, y_j) x_i y_j \qquad (1.11)$$

If X and Y are independent, then eq.1.11 can be written as

$$E[XY] = \sum_{i=1}^{m} x_i p(x_i) \sum_{j=1}^{n} y_j p(y_j) = E[X]E[Y] \qquad (1.12)$$

Thus, the expectation of the product of two independent random variables is the product of their expectations. If the two variables are dependent, then it is generally not possible to express the expectation of their product in this way.

The expectation of X^n is

$$E[X^n] = \sum_{i=1}^{m} x_i^n p(x_i) \qquad (1.13)$$

If $g(X)$ is a function of X that has a Taylor series expansion (most functions that you will commonly deal with fall in this category) then, using eq.1.13 and the linearity property of the expectation, the expectation of $g(X)$ is

$$E[g(X)] = \sum_{i=1}^{m} g(x_i)p(x_i) \qquad (1.14)$$

1.4 Variance and Standard Deviation

The mean of a random variable does not tell the whole story. You also have to know how the values are distributed about the mean. Are most values very close to the mean, or are they spread out far from the mean? One way to measure how the values are distributed is to calculate what is called the variance. The variance of a random variable is usually given the symbol σ^2 and is calculated as follows

$$\sigma^2 = \text{Var}[X] = E[(X - \mu)^2] = \sum_{i=1}^{m} (x_i - \mu)^2 p(x_i) \quad (1.15)$$

The equation says that the variance is equal to the mean of the square of the differences between x_i and μ. The standard deviation is simply the square root of the variance

$$\sigma = \sqrt{\text{Var}[X]} = \sqrt{\sum_{i=1}^{m} (x_i - \mu)^2 p(x_i)} \qquad (1.16)$$

A random variable with a large variance or standard deviation will have values that can differ from the mean by a large amount. Eq.1.15 for the variance can also be written in the following form

$$\text{Var}[X] = E[X^2] - E^2[X] = E[x^2] - \mu^2 \qquad (1.17)$$

where

$$E[X^2] = \sum_{i=1}^{m} x_i^2 p(x_i) \qquad (1.18)$$

is the expectation of the square of X.

Derivation of eq.1.17.
Expanding the squared term in eq.1.15 gives

$$
\begin{aligned}
\text{Var}[X] &= \sum_{i=1}^{m} (x_i^2 - 2\mu x_i + \mu^2) p(x_i) \\
&= E[X^2] - 2\mu E[x] + \mu^2 \\
&= E[X^2] - 2\mu^2 + \mu^2 \\
&= E[X^2] - \mu^2
\end{aligned}
$$

The variance of the sum of two random variables is defined as follows

$$
\begin{aligned}
\mathrm{Var}[X+Y] &= E[(X-\mu_x+Y-\mu_y)^2] & (1.19)\\
&= E[(X-\mu_x)^2 + 2(X-\mu_x)(Y-\mu_y) + (Y-\mu_y)^2]\\
&= E[(X-\mu_x)^2] + E[(Y-\mu_y)^2]\\
&\quad + 2E[(X-\mu_x)(Y-\mu_y)]\\
&= \mathrm{Var}[X] + \mathrm{Var}[Y] + 2\mathrm{Cov}[X,Y]
\end{aligned}
$$

The variance of the sum is equal to the sum of the variances plus two times a term called the covariance of the two random variables. The covariance is defined as follows.

$$
\begin{aligned}
\mathrm{Cov}[X,Y] &= E[(X-\mu_x)(Y-\mu_y)] & (1.20)\\
&= E[XY - X\mu_y - Y\mu_x + \mu_x\mu_y]\\
&= E[XY] - \mu_y E[X] - \mu_x E[Y] + \mu_x\mu_y\\
&= E[XY] - \mu_y\mu_x - \mu_x\mu_y + \mu_x\mu_y\\
&= E[XY] - \mu_x\mu_y
\end{aligned}
$$

If X and Y are independent then eq.1.12 says that $E[XY] = \mu_x\mu_y$ which makes the covariance zero. The variance of the sum of two independent random variables is then just equal to the sum of their variances.

1.5   Chebyshev's Theorem

The mean of a random variable gives you a central value around which the random values of the variable cluster.

The variance and standard deviation tell you how much on average that the values deviate from the mean. The next obvious question to ask is what is the probability that a value will be within a given distance of the mean. That question can be partly answered by Chebyshev's Theorem which says that the probability that a random variable, with mean μ and variance σ^2, assumes a value within a distance $\Delta \geq \sigma$ from the mean obeys the following

$$P(\mu - \Delta < X < \mu + \Delta) \geq 1 - \frac{\sigma^2}{\Delta^2} \qquad (1.21)$$

This inequality gives you a lower limit on the probability. It says that the probability that X is within the given range is at least as large as $1 - \sigma^2/\Delta^2$.

The amazing thing about Chebyshev's Theorem is that it is independent of the probability distribution. For example if you want the probability that a random variable is within two standard deviations from the mean then $\Delta = 2\sigma$ and eq.1.21 is

$$P(\mu - 2\sigma < X < \mu + 2\sigma) \geq 1 - \frac{\sigma^2}{4\sigma^2} = \frac{3}{4} \qquad (1.22)$$

Note that we do not need to know what the probability distribution of X is in order to get this result.

Chebyshev's Theorem is useful for comparing some of the simple gambling systems presented in the next chapter. Below is a proof of the theorem for the curious. Feel free to skip it if you like.

Proof of Chebyshev's Theorem.

First note that

$$P(\mu - \Delta < X < \mu + \Delta) = P(|X - \mu| < \Delta)$$
$$= 1 - P(|X - \mu| \geq \Delta)$$

Now recall the definition of variance

$$\sigma^2 = \sum_{x_i} (x_i - \mu)^2 p(x_i)$$

where the sum is over all the x_i.

If you only sum over those x_i such that $|x_i - \mu| \geq \Delta$ then obviously

$$\sigma^2 \geq \sum_{|x_i - \mu| \geq \Delta} (x_i - \mu)^2 p(x_i) \geq \sum_{|x_i - \mu| \geq \Delta} \Delta^2 p(x_i)$$

and

$$\sum_{|x_i - \mu| \geq \Delta} \Delta^2 p(x_i) = \Delta^2 P(|X - \mu| \geq \Delta)$$

Therefore

$$P(|X - \mu| \geq \Delta) \leq \frac{\sigma^2}{\Delta^2}$$

Using this in the first expression above gives

$$P(\mu - \Delta < X < \mu + \Delta) \geq 1 - \frac{\sigma^2}{\Delta^2}$$

■

1.6 Moment Generating Functions

It is sometimes necessary to calculate what are called the moments of a random variable. The nth moment of a random variable X is the expectation of X^n

$$E[X^n] = \sum_{i=1}^{m} x_i^n p(x_i) \qquad (1.23)$$

In particular $E[X^2]$ is required to calculate the variance of X

$$\text{Var}[X] = E[X^2] - E^2[X] \qquad (1.24)$$

In some cases where eq.1.23 is difficult to evaluate, it may be possible to use what is called a moment generating function. The moment generating function for X is defined as

$$M_x(s) = E[e^{Xs}] = \sum_{i=1}^{m} e^{x_i s} p(x_i) \qquad (1.25)$$

To get the nth moment from this function, first take the nth derivative with respect to s

$$\frac{d^n M_x(t)}{ds^n} = \sum_{i=1}^{m} x_i^n e^{x_i s} p(x_i) \qquad (1.26)$$

then set $s = 0$ to get the nth moment.

There may be situations where it is easier to evaluate $M_x(s)$ in closed form than it is to evaluate eq.1.23.

1.7 Binary Random Variables

A binary random variable can have only two possible values. Call the probabilities of the two values p and q. Since there are only two values, $p + q = 1$. If X is a binary random variable with values x_1 and x_2 then the expectation of X is

$$E[X] = x_1 p + x_2 q = (x_1 - x_2)p + x_2 \qquad (1.27)$$

The classic use of a binary random variable is to represent a coin toss. The value of x_1 could be used to represent the occurrence of heads and x_2 the occurrence of tails. The numeric values assigned to x_1 and x_2 will depend on what the random variable is being used for.

If you simply want X to indicate the occurrence of heads then set $x_1 = 1$ and $x_2 = 0$. The expectation in this case is $E[X] = p$. If you want X to represent the random gain or loss of some amount, such as in a coin toss bet, then set $x_1 = 1$ and $x_2 = -1$. The expectation in this case is $E[X] = 2p - 1$. This example will be discussed in more detail later.

1.8 Binomial Random Variable

When you add two or more binary random variables you get a binomial random variable. Consider for example tossing a coin n times and let X_i be the binary random variable that represents the ith toss. Let $X_i = 1$ indicate heads and $X_i = 0$ indicate tails, then summing all of the X_i gives you a random variable that indicates the number of times that heads occurs in the n tosses. Call the variable Y so that

$$Y = \sum_{i=1}^{n} X_i \qquad (1.28)$$

Y is a binomial random variable that can take on the values $0, 1, 2, \ldots, n$.

To calculate the probabilities for Y, recall first of all that the probability of two or more independent random variable events occurring is just the product of their individual probabilities. Since coin tosses are independent, the probability of a particular sequence of tosses, where heads occurs k times and tails $n-k$ times, is equal to $p^k(1-p)^{n-k}$, where p is the probability of heads and $1-p = q$ is the probability of tails on any one of the tosses. The number of ways of getting k heads in n tosses is the same as the number of ways of selecting k objects (tosses) from a set of n objects (tosses) when the order does not matter. This number is given by the binomial coefficient

$$\binom{n}{k} = \frac{n!}{k!(n-k)!} \tag{1.29}$$

Each of these ways has the probability given above, therefore the probability that $Y = k$ is

$$P(Y = k) = p^k(1-p)^{n-k}\binom{n}{k} \tag{1.30}$$

This is called a binomial probability distribution. The name comes from the fact that these probabilities are equal to the terms in the expansion of the binomial $(p+q)^n$

$$(p+q)^n = \sum_{k=0}^{n} p^k q^{n-k}\binom{n}{k} \tag{1.31}$$

Since $p + q = 1$ you can see that the probabilities all sum to 1 as they should.

The mean of Y can easily be calculated from eq.1.28

$$
\begin{aligned}
E[Y] &= \sum_{i=1}^{n} E[x_i] \\
&= \sum_{i=1}^{n} p \\
&= np
\end{aligned}
\tag{1.32}
$$

The variance can be calculated in the same way

$$\text{Var}[Y] = \sum_{i=1}^{n} \text{Var}[x_i] \qquad (1.33)$$
$$= \sum_{i=1}^{n} pq$$
$$= npq$$

When n gets large and p is not close to 1 or 0 then the binomial distribution can be approximated by a continuous probability distribution called a normal distribution.

A continuous random variable Y_c that has a normal distribution with mean μ and variance σ^2 has probabilities given by

$$P(y_1 < Y_c < y_2) = \frac{1}{\sqrt{2\pi\sigma^2}} \int_{y_1}^{y_2} \exp\left(\frac{-(y-\mu)^2}{2\sigma^2}\right) dy$$
$$(1.34)$$

If you let $\mu = np$ and $\sigma^2 = npq$ then Y_c can be used to approximate the binomial random variable Y. Figure 1.2 shows an example of a binomial distribution with $n = 20$, $p = 0.5$, and its normal distribution approximation with $\mu = np = 10$, and $\sigma^2 = npq = 5$.

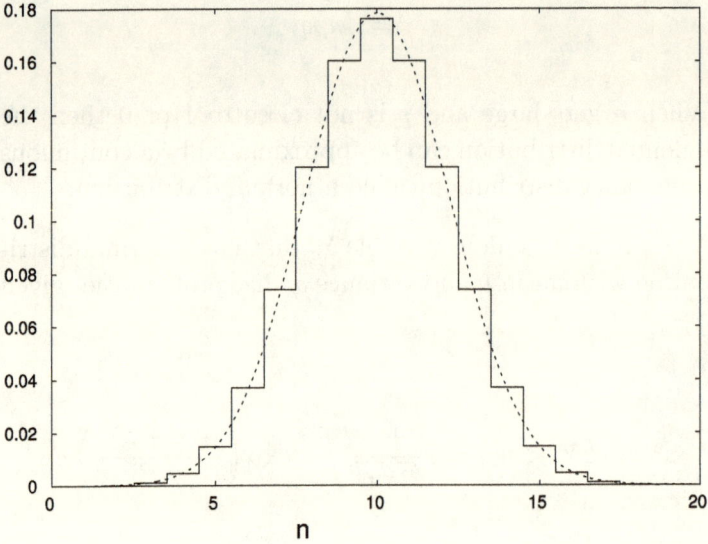

Figure 1.2: Binomial distribution with $n = 20$, $p = 0.5$, and its normal distribution approximation with $\mu = np = 10$, and $\sigma^2 = npq = 5$.

This page intentionally left blank.

Now we can begin our investigation.

Chapter 2

Gambling Systems

In this chapter we will look at gambling systems where the
size of a bet is a function only of the wins, losses, and sizes
of previous bets. The size of the bankroll plays no roll in
determining the size of the bet in these systems. This is
a serious disadvantage with the result that it is easy to
go bankrupt (bankroll=0) using these systems. We only
consider the simplest gambling situation where there are
only two possible outcomes: you either lose the amount
of your bet or you win the amount. There are only two
possible returns in this case, +1 or -1, corresponding to a
100% gain or loss.

2.1   General Framework

To develop a general framework for analyzing gambling systems, start by defining the following variables.

$$
\begin{aligned}
a_n &= \text{bankroll at the } n^{th} \text{ bet} \\
b_n &= \text{size of the } n^{th} \text{ bet} \\
x_n &= \begin{cases} +1 & \text{with probability} = p \text{ (win)} \\ -1 & \text{with probability} = 1 - p = q \text{ (loss)} \end{cases}
\end{aligned}
$$

x_n is a binary random variable that represents the win or loss of the nth bet. The bankroll satisfies the following stochastic difference equation.

$$a_{n+1} = a_n + x_n b_n \tag{2.1}$$

To find the bankroll expectation start by taking the expectation of this equation

$$E[a_{n+1}] = E[a_n] + E[x_n b_n] \tag{2.2}$$

x_n and b_n must be independent therefore

$$E[x_n b_n] = E[x_n] E[b_n] \tag{2.3}$$

$E[x_n]$ can easily be calculated as follows

$$E[x_n] = p - q = 2p - 1 \qquad (2.4)$$

Substituting this into eq.2.2 gives

$$E[a_{n+1}] = E[a_n] + (2p - 1)E[b_n] \qquad (2.5)$$

The initial bankroll, a_0, is given so that $E[a_0] = a_0$. The solution to eq.2.5 can therefor be expressed as

$$E[a_n] = a_0 + (2p - 1) \sum_{i=0}^{n-1} E[b_i] \qquad (2.6)$$

It is often times more convenient to work with the equation in this form

$$E[t_n] = (2p - 1) \sum_{i=0}^{n-1} E[b_i] \qquad (2.7)$$

where $t_n = a_n - a_0$ is the tally of all the wins and losses up to the nth bet. You can also think of t_n as the bankroll you would have if your initial bankroll was zero.

There is another way to calculate $E[t_n]$. Let $S_n(k)$ be the sum of the tallies for all series of n bets for which k wins occur, then since each of these tallies has the probability $p^k(1 - p)^{n-k}$, the expectation can be expressed as

$$E[t_n] = \sum_{k=0}^{n} S_n(k)p^k(1-p)^{n-k} \qquad (2.8)$$

It may be easier to use eq.2.7 or 2.8 depending on the difficulty of determining $E[b_i]$ or $S_n(k)$. Examples will be given for using each.

The variance of t_n is given by

$$\mathrm{Var}[t_n] = E[t_n^2] - E^2[t_n] \qquad (2.9)$$

To calculate $E[t_n^2]$ you can use an equation like eq.2.8 where $S_n(k)$ in this case would be the sum of the squares of the tallies. In some cases it may also be possible to use a moment generating function as discussed previously.

2.2   Single State System

The simplest betting system consists of just betting the same amount every time. We will call this a single state system. To simplify things, let the size of each bet equal 1 so that $b_i = 1$, $E[b_i] = 1$ and eq.2.7 becomes

$$E[t_n] = (2p - 1)\sum_{i=0}^{n-1} 1 = (2p - 1)n \qquad (2.10)$$

Now let's calculate the same thing using eq.2.8. The tally

for any series of n bets in which k wins occurs is $2k - n$ and there will be $\binom{n}{k}$ such series so that

$$S_n(k) = (2k - n)\binom{n}{k} \tag{2.11}$$

Eq.2.8 then becomes

$$E[t_n] = \sum_{k=0}^{n}(2k - n)\binom{n}{k}p^k(1 - p)^{n-k} \tag{2.12}$$

This looks almost like the expansion of the binomial $(p + q)^n$. First write the equation as

$$E[t_n] = 2\sum_{k=0}^{n}k\binom{n}{k}p^kq^{n-k} - n\sum_{k=0}^{n}\binom{n}{k}p^kq^{n-k} \tag{2.13}$$

The second summation is the expansion of $(p + q)^n = 1$. The first summation can be written as

$$\begin{aligned}
p\frac{d}{dp}\sum_{k=0}^{n}\binom{n}{k}p^kq^{n-k} &= p\frac{d}{dp}(p + q)^n \tag{2.14}\\
&= pn(p + q)^{n-1}\\
&= pn
\end{aligned}$$

Substituting this into eq.2.13 gives

$$E[t_n] = 2pn - n = (2p - 1)n \qquad (2.15)$$

which agrees with eq.2.10. In this case, using eq.2.8 to calculate $E[t_n]$ is significantly more difficult than using eq.2.7 but this may not always be the case.

To calculate the variance of t_n you need $E[t_n^2]$. This can be calculated similar to eq.2.12

$$E[t_n^2] = \sum_{k=0}^{n} (2k - n)^2 \binom{n}{k} p^k (1 - p)^{n-k} \qquad (2.16)$$

Evaluating this sum can be done, but it is somewhat tedious (give it a try). In this case, it is easier to use a moment generating function

$$
\begin{aligned}
M_{t_n}(s) &= E[e^{t_n s}] \qquad (2.17) \\
&= \sum_{k=0}^{n} e^{(2k-n)s} \binom{n}{k} p^k (1 - p)^{n-k} \\
&= e^{-ns} \sum_{k=0}^{n} \binom{n}{k} (pe^{2s})^k q^{n-k} \\
&= e^{-ns} (pe^{2s} + q)^n = (pe^s + qe^{-s})^n
\end{aligned}
$$

Now $E[t_n^2]$ can be evaluated as follows

$$E[t_n^2] = \frac{d^2 M_{t_n}(s)}{ds^2}\bigg|_{s=0} = n(n - 1)(p - q)^2 + n \qquad (2.18)$$

The variance is then

$$\text{Var}[t_n] = E[t_n^2] - E^2[t_n] = 4npq = 4np(1-p) \quad (2.19)$$

Note that you can also use the above moment generating function to calculate $E[t_n]$.

2.3 Two State System

Now we want to look at a sligthly more complicated system called a two state system. In this system you use one bet when winning and another bet when losing. You start off betting an amount β_1. If you win, then you keep betting β_1. If you lose, then you switch to betting β_2. If you're betting β_2 and you lose again, you stay with β_2, otherwise if you win you switch back to β_1. The process is illustrated in figure 2.1.

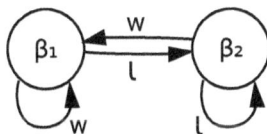

Figure 2.1: Two state system transition diagram

The circled β_1 and β_2 represent the two bets (states) and the arrows represent the transition between the states. The arrow labeled l represents what to do when you lose, and the arrow labeled w represents what to do when you win.

To calculate the expected tally, it is easiest to use the formula involving the expected bet. There are only two possible values of the nth bet, β_1 and β_2, so the bet expectation is (note $E[b_0] = \beta_1$)

$$E[b_n] = \beta_1 P(\beta_1) + \beta_2 P(\beta_2) \qquad (2.20)$$

Betting β_1 depends only on the probability of the previous bet being a win so $P(\beta_1) = p$. Betting β_2 depends only on the probability of the previous bet being a loss so $P(\beta_2) = q$. Therefore eq.2.20 is just

$$E[b_n] = \beta_1 p + \beta_2 q \qquad (2.21)$$

and the expected tally is (using eq.2.7)

$$
\begin{aligned}
E[t_n] &= (2p-1) \sum_{i=0}^{n-1} E[b_n] \qquad (2.22)\\
&= (2p-1)\left[\beta_1 + (\beta_1 p + \beta_2 q)(n-1)\right]
\end{aligned}
$$

How does this compare with the single state system that uses β_1 for all bets? The expectation for the single state system is

$$E[t_n] = (2p-1)\beta_1 n \qquad (2.23)$$

Subtracting eq.2.23 from 2.22 gives the difference in expectations for the two systems

$$\Delta = (2p - 1)q(\beta_2 - \beta_1)(n - 1) \qquad (2.24)$$

Assuming that $p > \frac{1}{2}$ so that you have better than even odds of winning, the two state system will have a larger expectation if your losing bet is larger than your winning bet, i.e. $\beta_2 > \beta_1$.

The variance for the general two state system is a bit tedious to derive. We will simply state the result for the special case where $\beta_1 = 1$ and $\beta_2 = 2$.

$$Var[t_n] = \begin{cases} 4pq & n = 1 \\ 4pq^2 \left((5 - 3n)p + 6n - 7\right) + pq(n + 3) & n > 1 \end{cases}$$
$$\qquad (2.25)$$

The expectation formula in this case is

$$E[t_n] = (2p - 1)\left(1 + (2 - p)(n - 1)\right) \qquad (2.26)$$

Figure 2.2 shows the variance versus mean for the two state, and single state systems with $\beta_1 = 1$, $\beta_2 = 2$, and $p = 0.6$. Note the linear relationship between variance and mean, which is due to the fact that n appears only to the first power in eqs.2.15 and eqs.2.19 of the single state system, and eqs.2.25 and 2.26 of the two state system. The single state system has a smaller slope.

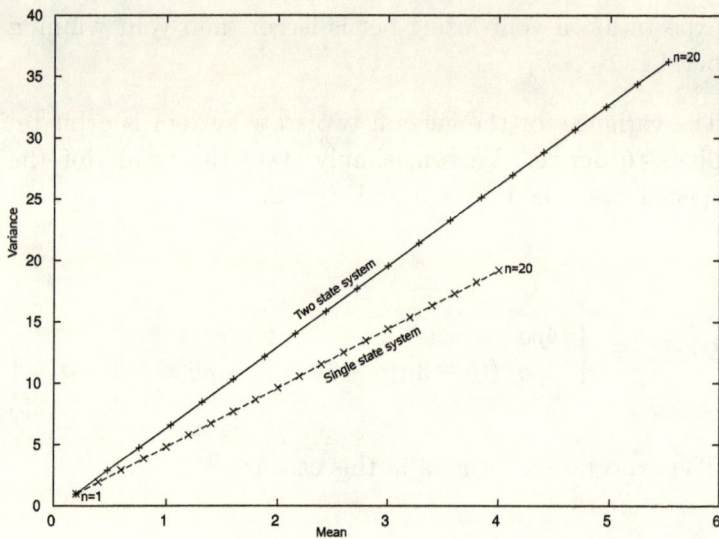

Figure 2.2: Variance versus mean for the two state and single state systems, with number of bets $= n = 1, 2, \ldots, 20$, and $p = 0.6$.

2.4 m State System

An obvious generalization of the two state system is to the case where you have m states with bets β_i, $i = 1, 2, \ldots m$. The way the system works is as follows. If you are in state i (betting β_i) and you lose, then you switch to state $i + 1$ unless $i = m$ in which case you stay in state m. If you win, then you switch to state $i - 1$ unless $i = 1$ in which case you stay in state 1. The state diagram for this system is shown in figure 2.3.

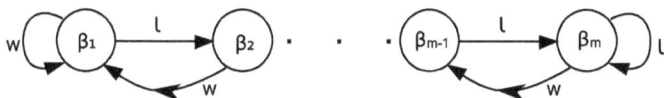

Figure 2.3: m state system transition diagram

Simple formulas for the expectation and variance of this general system do not exist but they can be calculated algorithmically. Below is a function in the Python programming language that will return the expectation and variance for the m state system where $\beta_i = i$.

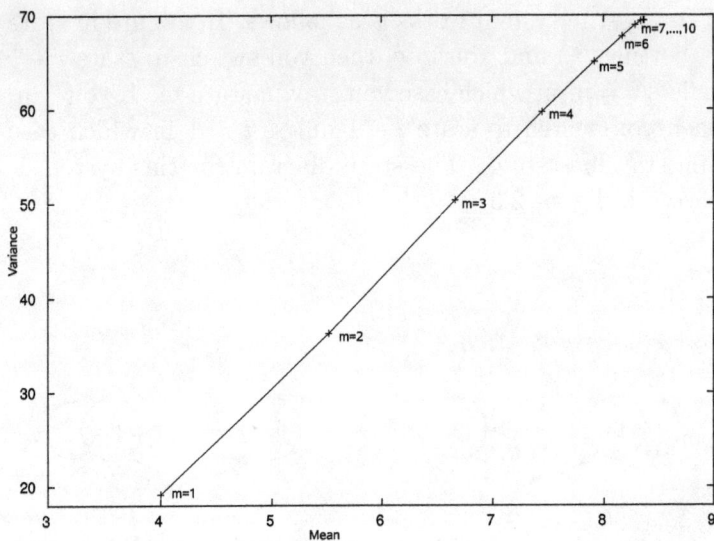

Figure 2.4: Variance versus mean for m state systems, with $m = 1, 2, \ldots, 10$, probability of winning= 0.6, number of bets= 20.

```
def evn_mstate(m,p,n):
    """
    m state system statistics.
    Returns the mean and variance for playing the m state system
    n times.
    m = number of states
    p = win probability
    n = number of bets
    """
    e = 0    # mean
    e2 = 0   # second moment
    for g in xrange(0,pow(2,n)):
        t = 0  # running tally
        w = 0  # win counter
        l = 0  # loss counter
        b = 1  # bet amount
        for i in xrange(0,n):
            if (g >> i) & 1:
                w += 1
                t += b
                if b > 1: b -= 1
            else:
                l += 1
                t -= b
                if b < m: b += 1
        prb = pow(p,w) * pow(1-p,l)
        e += t * prb
        e2 += t * t * prb
    v = e2 - e * e # calculate variance
    return (e,v)
```

Figure 2.4 shows the variance versus mean for m state systems where m ranges from 1 to 10.

2.5   Martingale System

In the Martingale system you start out with some initial bet and every time you lose, you multiply the bet by a constant factor to get the size of your next bet. When you win you go back to your initial bet amount. The most common factor used is 2. If you start out betting \$1 and you double your bet every time you lose then you will come out 1 unit ahead on the next win. The process is illustrated in figure 2.5.

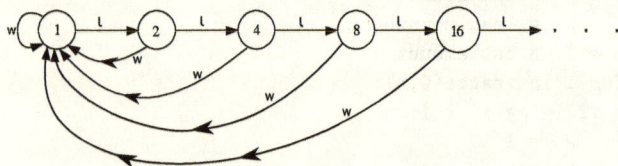

Figure 2.5: Martingale state transition diagram

In general let the bet multiplication factor be r then after losing a string of k bets your total loss will be

$$\sum_{i=0}^{k-1} r^i = \frac{r^k - 1}{r - 1} \qquad (2.27)$$

Winning the next bet then means gaining r^k units for a net of

$$r^k - \left(\frac{r^k - 1}{r - 1}\right) = \frac{r^k(r - 2) + 1}{r - 1} \qquad (2.28)$$

For $r = 2$ this reduces to just 1. For an example with $r = 3$, suppose you lose 3 bets in a row and then win the 4th. Your total losses will be

$$1 + 3 + 9 = \frac{3^3 - 1}{3 - 1} = 13$$

On the 4th bet you will win $3^3 = 27$ units for a net gain of $27 - 13 = 14$ units. You can also calculate this directly using eq.2.28 with $r = 3$ and $k = 3$.

To calculate the expected tally for n bets it is easiest to use eq.2.7 in this case. The possible values of the nth bet are, $b_n = r^j$, $j = 0, 1, 2, \ldots, n$ (note that the initial, or zeroth bet, is always equal to 1, $b_0 = 1$). The expectation is then

$$E[b_n] = \sum_{j=0}^{n} r^j p(r^j) \tag{2.29}$$

For the bet to equal r^j with $j < n$, there has to be a win followed by j losses in a row which has a probability of pq^j. For the bet to equal r^n all bets must have been losses which has a probability of q^n. Eq.2.29 then becomes

$$E[b_n] = p\sum_{j=0}^{n-1}(rq)^j + (rq)^n \tag{2.30}$$

$$= p\frac{(1-(rq)^n)}{1-rq} + (rq)^n$$

$$= \frac{p-(r-1)q(rq)^n}{1-rq}$$

The tally expectation is then

$$E[t_n] = \frac{2p-1}{1-rq}\sum_{j=0}^{n-1}(p-(r-1)q(rq)^j) \tag{2.31}$$

$$= \frac{2p-1}{1-rq}\left[pn-(r-1)q\left(\frac{1-(rq)^n}{1-rq}\right)\right]$$

Note once again that when $p = \frac{1}{2}$, $E[t_n] = 0$ so that the Martingale will get you nowhere on average, regardless of the multiplication factor, r.

In the most common Martingale system, $r = 2$, so that you double your bet each time you lose. With $r = 2$ eq.2.31 becomes

$$E[t_n] = pn - q\left(\frac{1-(2q)^n}{1-2q}\right) \tag{2.32}$$

The variance of the Martingale system is somewhat more difficult to calculate. We will only calculate it for the case of $r = 2$.

To calculate the variance, we need to find the expectation of the squares of the tallys. First we need to determine what the final tallys are. For n bets with no wins, the final tally will be $1 - 2^n$ with probability $q^n = (1 - p)^n$. For n bets with k wins, where $k = 1, 2, 3, \ldots n$, the final tally will have one of the following possible values

$$k + 1 - 2^{j-1} \qquad j = 1, 2, 3, \ldots n - k + 1 \qquad (2.33)$$

Each of these values will occur $\binom{n-j}{k-1}$ times and with probability $p^k q^{n-k}$. Using these values, the expectation is

$$E[t_n^2] = (1-2^n)^2 q^n + \sum_{k=1}^{n} p^k q^{n-k} \sum_{j=1}^{n-k+1} \binom{n-j}{k-1}(k+1-2^{j-1})^2$$

$$(2.34)$$

The variance is then simply

$$\mathrm{Var}[t_n] = E[t_n^2] - E^2[t_n]$$

where the tally expectation is given by eq.2.32.

Figure 2.6 shows the log(variance) versus mean for the Martingale system with multiplication factors $r = 1.6, 1.8, 2.0$, probability of winning $= 0.6$, and number of bets $= 1, 2, \ldots, 20$. Note the log scale on the vertical, signifying that the variance grows very rapidly with respect to the mean.

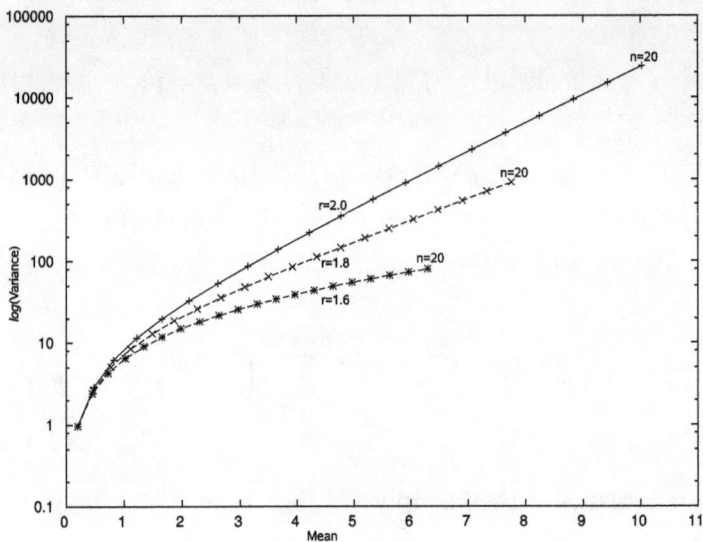

Figure 2.6: log(variance) versus mean for Martingale system, with multiplication factor $= r = 1.6, 1.8, 2.0$, number of bets $= n = 1, 2, \ldots, 20$, and probability of winning $= 0.6$.

2.6 Cancellation System

A simple cancellation betting system keeps a list of the amount of each lost bet. A new bet is constructed by adding 1 to the last entry in the lost bet list, i.e. the amount of the most recently lost bet. If the lost bet list is empty, the new bet is just equal to 1. If the new bet is won, then the last entry in the lost bet list is removed and the process starts over. If the new bet is lost then its amount is added to the lost bet list and the process starts over. The Python code for calculating the expectation and variance for this system is shown below.

```python
def evn_cancel(p,n):
    """
    Cancellation system statistics
    Returns the mean and variance for playing the
    Cancellation system n times.
    p = win probability
    n = number of bets
    """
    e = 0    # mean
    e2 = 0   # second moment
    for g in xrange(0,pow(2,n)):
        t = 0   # running tally
        w = 0   # win counter
        l = 0   # loss counter
        ll = [] # loss list
        for i in xrange(0,n):
            b = 1
            if len(ll): b+=ll[len(ll)-1]
            if (g >> i) & 1:
                w += 1
                t += b
                if len(ll): ll.pop()
```

```
    else:
        l += 1
        t -= b
        ll.append(b)
    prb = pow(p,w) * pow(1-p,l)
    e += t * prb
    e2 += t * t * prb
  v = e2 - e * e # calculate variance
  return (e,v)
```

Figure 2.7 shows the variance versus mean for the cancellation system, and the two state system for comparison, with probability of winning $= 0.6$, and number of bets $= 1, 2, \ldots, 20$. Note the linear relationship between the variance and the mean.

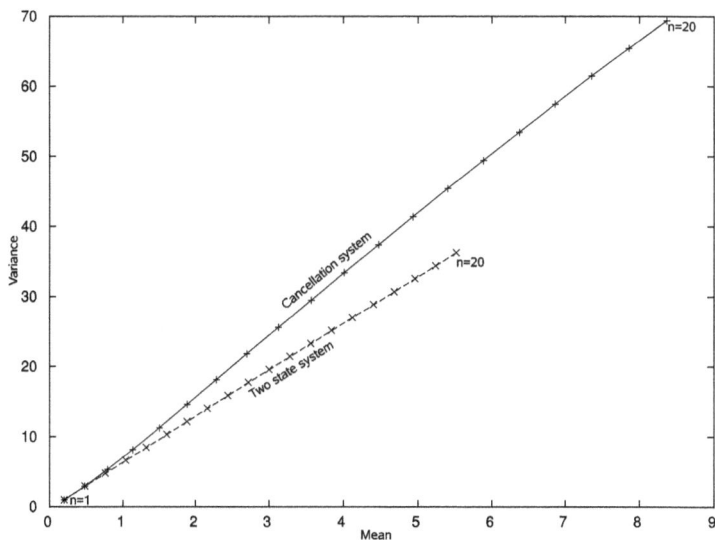

Figure 2.7: Variance versus mean for cancellation system, with number of bets $= n = 1, 2, \ldots, 20$, and probability of winning $= 0.6$.

On to the crust of the matter.

Chapter 3

The Kelly System

3.1 Fixed Fraction Betting

All the betting systems we have looked at so far are similar
in the sense that bets are only determined by the sizes of
previous bets and/or whether the previous bets were won
or lost. The size of the bankroll played no part in deciding
the size of the bet. Now we want to look at a system where
the size of the bet is determined solely by the current size
of ones bankroll.

The simplest way to base a bet on the size of your bankroll,
is to make the bet equal to a fixed fraction of the bankroll.
If f is the bankroll fraction, then the nth bet will be $b_n = fa_n$, and the general gambling equation, eq.2.1, becomes

$$a_{n+1} = (1 + x_n f)a_n \qquad (3.1)$$

Using a_0 as the initial bankroll, this equation can be iterated to give

$$a_n = a_0 \prod_{i=0}^{n-1} (1 + x_i f) \qquad (3.2)$$

The initial bankroll a_0 is just a scale factor in this equation and can be set equal to 1. You can also think of this as dividing the equation through by a_0 and then using a scaled bankroll a_n/a_0. In either case we will drop the a_0 term from here on so that eq.3.2 becomes

$$a_n = \prod_{i=0}^{n-1} (1 + x_i f) \qquad (3.3)$$

The expectation of a_n is easy to calculate since the x_i random variables are independent and therefore the expectation of the product is equal to the product of the expectations

$$E[a_n] = \prod_{i=0}^{n-1} E[1 + x_i f] \qquad (3.4)$$

The product expectations are all identical and equal to

$$E[1 + x_i f] = p(1 + f) + (1 - p)(1 - f) \qquad (3.5)$$
$$= 1 + (2p - 1)f$$

The bankroll expectation then becomes

$$E[a_n] = (1 + (2p - 1)f)^n \qquad (3.6)$$

Note that for even odds of winning or losing, $p = \frac{1}{2}$, the expectation reduces to $E[a_n] = 1$, meaning that on average you will get nowhere, as you should expect.

To calculate the variance of a_n, it is easier to first put eq.3.3 in a different form. Instead of using the random variables x_i, you can use the single random variable k that represents the number of wins in a series of n bets. Clearly k can have the values $k = 0, 1, 2, \ldots n$ with probabilities $p^k q^{n-k} = p^k (1-p)^{n-k}$. In eq.3.3, where there is a win $x_i = 1$ and when there is a loss $x_i = -1$ so that the alternative form of the equation is

$$a_n = (1 + f)^k (1 - f)^{n-k} \qquad (3.7)$$

For the variance, the expectation of a_n^2 needs to be calculated. Using eq.3.7, the expectation is

$$E[a_n^2] = \sum_{k=0}^{n} \binom{n}{k} (1 + f)^{2k} (1 - f)^{2n-2k} p^k q^{n-k} \qquad (3.8)$$

This can be rewritten as follows

$$E[a_n^2] = \sum_{k=0}^{n} \binom{n}{k} \left((1+f)^2 p\right)^k \left((1-f)^2 q\right)^{n-k} \qquad (3.9)$$

The summation can now be recognized as a binomial expansion so that the equation simplifies to

$$\begin{aligned} E[a_n^2] &= \left((1+f)^2 p + (1-f)^2 q\right)^n \qquad (3.10) \\ &= \left(4fp + (1-f)^2\right)^n \end{aligned}$$

The variance is then

$$\begin{aligned} \mathrm{Var}[a_n] &= E[a_n^2] - E^2[a_n] \qquad (3.11) \\ &= \left(4fp + (1-f)^2\right)^n - \left(1 + (2p-1)f\right)^{2n} \\ &= \left(f^2 + 2(2p-1)f + 1\right)^n \\ &\quad - \left(f^2(2p-1)^2 + 2(2p-1)f + 1\right)^n \end{aligned}$$

3.2   Choosing a Fixed Fraction

The unsolved problem of the fixed fraction betting system is how to choose the fraction f. If your goal is to maximize the expectation in eq.3.6 then the obvious choice is to let $f = 1$. This means betting your entire bankroll at each bet. The problem with this is easy to see, a single loss and you are wiped out. Clearly then it is best to use a fraction less than 1.

Is there a way to objectively choose a value of f that is optimal for a given game with a probability p of winning? The answer is yes and there are two ways to approach the problem. Both ways are equivalent in the end, but they begin by looking at the problem from two very different points of view. We will briefly describe both approaches.

3.2.1 The Bernoulli Approach

The Bernoulli approach uses what is called risk aversion or utility theory. This is a broad subject and we will not cover it in detail here. The general idea is that instead of trying to maximize the expectation of a_n, we try to maximize the expectation of a function of a_n. This function is called a utility function and it must have the property of being an increasing continuous function. This means that if $U(x)$ is a utility function and $x_2 > x_1$, then $U(x_2) > U(x_1)$. The variable x represents an amount of wealth, money or in our case bankroll, a_n, and the value $U(x)$ represents the desirability (or utility) of the amount. The simple condition that $U(x)$ must satisfy is another way of saying that a larger bankroll must always be more desirable than a smaller bankroll.

There are many possible choices for $U(x)$ but the one we will be interested in is $U(x) = \log x$. A plot of this function is shown in figure 3.1 where the base of the logarithm is

$e = 2.718\ldots$ (other bases can be used). The plot indicates that there is a diminishing increase in utility as x increases.

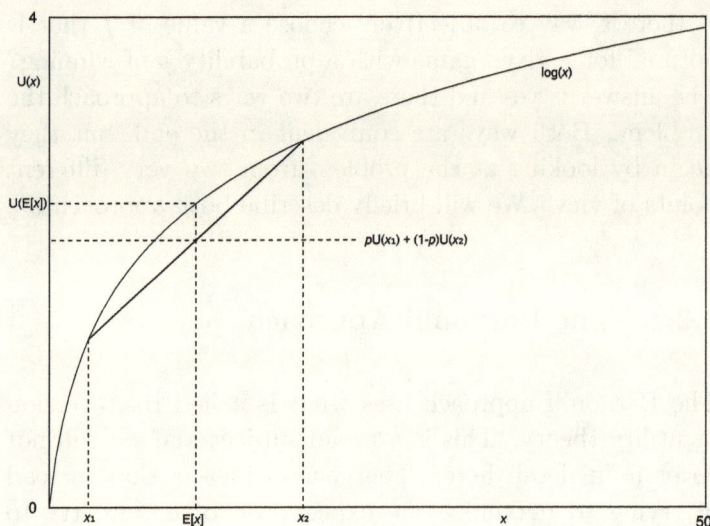

Figure 3.1: $U(x) = \log x$ shows a diminishing increase in utility as x increases.

Any utility function with this property of a diminishing increase in utility for increasing x is called risk averse. Mathematically, a function is risk averse if its second derivative is less than zero, $U''(x) < 0$.

The risk aversion property can be illustrated in terms of a game where the wealth outcome is x_1 with probability p and $x_2 > x_1$, with probability $q = 1 - p$ so that the expectation is

$$E[x] = px_1 + (1 - p)x_2 \qquad (3.12)$$

A utility function is then risk averse if the following condition holds

$$U(px_1 + (1 - p)x_2) > pU(x_1) + (1 - p)U(x_2) \qquad (3.13)$$

In other words, the utility of the expectation must be greater than the expectation of the utilities. As you can see in figure 3.1, $U(x) = \log x$ satisfies this condition.

Using a log utility function for the fixed fraction betting problem means that instead of trying to maximize the expectation of a_n, we want to maximize the expectation of $\log a_n$. Using eq.3.7 for a_n gives

$$\begin{aligned} E[\log a_n] &= E[k]\log(1 + f) \qquad (3.14) \\ &+ E[n - k]\log(1 - f) \end{aligned}$$

The expected number of wins is np so that this equation becomes

$$E[\log a_n] = n\left[p\log(1 + f) + (1 - p)\log(1 - f)\right] \qquad (3.15)$$

This is the expectation that needs to be maximized with respect to f in order to minimize the risk of having a_n go to

zero. We will show how to do this in the next section, but
first a historical note on the use of utility functions, and
then a description of the Kelly approach to this problem.

The first person to use $U(x) = \log x$ as a utility function was Daniel Bernoulli in 1738. He used it to resolve
a paradox that later became known as the St. Petersburg
paradox. This paradox is another example where basing
a decision on the expected value of some random outcome
is not always the most rational thing to do. The paradox
involves a game which has a payoff of 2^{k-1} if in a series of
coin flips, heads appears for the first time after k flips. For
a fair coin the payoff probability is $(\frac{1}{2})^k$ and the expected
payoff is

$$\sum_{k=1}^{\infty} 2^{k-1} \left(\frac{1}{2}\right)^k = \sum_{k=1}^{\infty} \frac{1}{2} = \infty \qquad (3.16)$$

The question is how much would you be willing to pay
to play this game? Basing your decision solely on the
expected payoff means you should be willing to pay any
amount to play since the expectation is infinite. Clearly
this is crazy and most people would only be willing to pay
a modest amount to play this game.

The solution to this paradox is to use the expected value
of the logarithm of the payoffs. If the base 2 logarithm is
used, then the expectation is

$$\sum_{k=1}^{\infty} \log_2(2^{k-1}) \left(\frac{1}{2}\right)^k = \sum_{k=1}^{\infty} \frac{k-1}{2^k} = 1 \qquad (3.17)$$

So according to this utility function you should not be willing to pay more than \$1 to play this game.

3.2.2 The Kelly Approach

Using a utility function to select an optimal betting fraction is not the only way to approach the problem. You could also look for a strategy that will make your bankroll grow the most in the long run. This is essentially the approach taken by a physicist named John Kelly working at Bell Labs. In 1956 he published a paper titled *A New Interpretation of Information Rate* in the *Bell System Technical Journal*. In the paper he determines the betting fraction through the goal of making the bankroll grow at the maximum possible exponential rate in the long run, i.e. as the number of bets becomes large. He also draws an interesting analogy between the exponential growth rate of the bankroll and the rate of information transmission through a communications channel.

Kelly's approach is to find the maximum exponential growth rate factor G, so that for a large number of bets n, the bankroll will grow as

$$a_n = a_0 e^{nG} \qquad (3.18)$$

The factor G is defined mathematically as the limit

$$G = \lim_{n \to \infty} \frac{1}{n} \log \left(\frac{a_n}{a_0} \right) \qquad (3.19)$$

To find this limit, Kelly used the expression for a_n in eq.3.7 (from here on assume $a_0 = 1$)

$$G = \lim_{n \to \infty} \left[\frac{k}{n} \log(1 + f) + \frac{n - k}{n} \log(1 - f) \right] \quad (3.20)$$

Now in the limit as n goes to infinity, the ratio k/n becomes the probability, p, of winning and $\frac{n-k}{n}$ becomes the probability, $1 - p = q$, of losing, so that eq.3.20 is

$$G = p \log(1 + f) + (1 - p) \log(1 - f) \quad (3.21)$$

Note that this is identical to the term in brackets in eq.3.15 which was arrived at from a utility function or risk aversion point of view. In the next section we will show how to maximize this equation with respect to f but first we want to give a short description of the analogy that Kelly drew between this problem and communication theory.

Imagine having a communication channel where you can learn the outcome of an event before it happens. The event could be a football game, a coin flip, a dice roll, or any other event that is normally unpredictable. With your communication channel you can place even money bets on the event and double your money every time by betting your entire bankroll. Now suppose the channel is noisy so that you receive the correct information about the outcome with a probability p, $\frac{1}{2} < p < 1$. You could still bet your entire bankroll which would give you an expectation

$$E[a_n] = (2p)^n \tag{3.22}$$

But you would go bankrupt with certainty if you play long enough since $p \neq 1$. The best you can do is bet a fraction f such that the exponential growth rate factor in eq.3.21 is maximized. It turns out that this maximum G is also exactly equal to the maximum rate at which information can be transmitted through your noisy channel. Mathematically we have

$$G_{max} = 1 - H(p) \tag{3.23}$$

where $H(p)$ is the entropy function for the channel. You can think of the entropy function as a measure of the amount of information received from a transmission through the channel. The entropy function will be discussed more in the next section.

Kelly therefore showed that a favorable bet can be modeled as a communications channel that provides prior information about the outcome of the bet, and the maximum bankroll growth rate is equivalent to the maximum rate at which information can be transmitted through the channel.

Both the Kelly and Bernoulli way of looking at this problem are useful and they both provide their own unique insights. In the end they both arrive at the same conclusion that the expectation of $\log a_n$ should be maximized. This system of betting should really be called the Bernoulli-Kelly system but it is most commonly called just the Kelly system which is the name we use in this book.

3.3   Expectation and Variance

The Kelly system is a fixed fraction betting system. The optimal fraction of bankroll to bet is found by maximizing the expectation of the logarithm of the bankroll (see previous section for a justification of this). This expectation is given by the following equation

$$E[\log a_n] = nG \tag{3.24}$$

where G is the long term exponential growth rate

$$G = p\log(1 + f) + (1 - p)\log(1 - f) \tag{3.25}$$

The goal then is to find the betting fraction f that maximizes G. The extrema (maximum or minimum points) of G with respect to f are those values of f for which the first derivative of G with respect to f is equal to zero. If you take the derivative of eq.3.25 with respect to f, set it equal to zero, and solve for f you find that there is only one extremum located at

$$f = 2p - 1 \tag{3.26}$$

Derivation of eq.3.26.

$$\frac{dG}{df} = \frac{p}{1+f} - \frac{1-p}{1-f} = 0$$
$$p(1-f) = (1-p)(1+f)$$
$$f = 2p - 1$$

To test if this is a maximum or minimum of G you evaluate the second derivative of G with respect to f at this point. If it is negative then you have a maximum and if positive then you have a minimum. Doing this gives

$$\frac{d^2G}{df^2} = -\frac{1}{4pq} \tag{3.27}$$

which is negative for all possible values of p and q. The value of f given by eq.3.26 therefore maximizes G. You can also see that G only has one maximum value by looking at figure 3.2 which shows a plot of G as a function of f for $p = 0.6, 0.7, 0.8$ using a base e logarithm.

If you substitute eq.3.26 into eq.3.25 you get the following expression for G

$$G = \log 2 - H(p) \tag{3.28}$$

where $H(p)$ is the binary entropy function given by

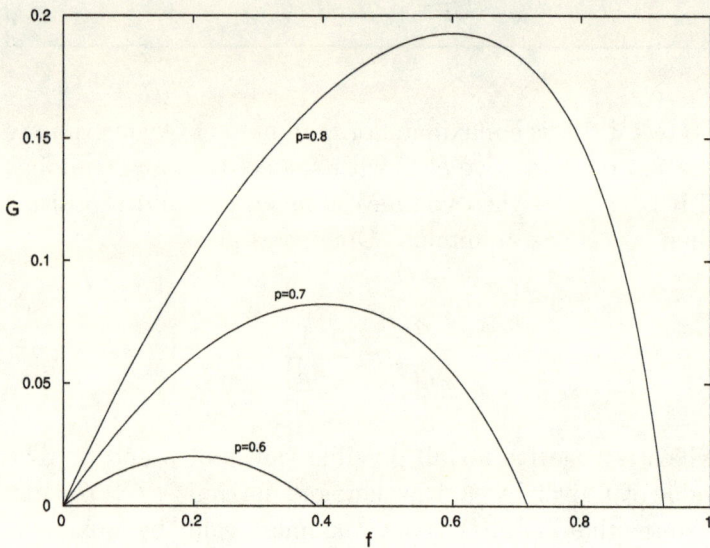

Figure 3.2: Exponential growth factor, G, as a function of betting fraction, f, for $p = 0.6, 0.7, 0.8$.

$$H(p) = -p \log p - (1 - p) \log(1 - p) \qquad (3.29)$$

You can think of $H(p)$ as measuring the amount of surprise or uncertainty associated with any process that has two possible outcomes which occur with probabilities p and $1 - p$. Figure 3.3 shows a plot of $H(p)$ using a base 2 logarithm. The values $p = 0$ or $p = 1$ correspond to one or the other of the outcomes occuring with certainty so that $H(p) = 0$ for these values. $H(p)$ has a maximum of 1 at $p = \frac{1}{2}$ which corresponds to maximum uncertainty, either outcome is equally likely.

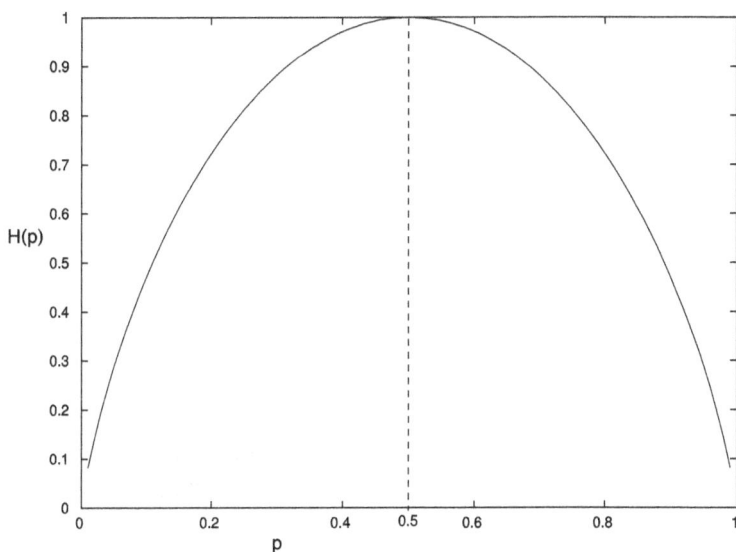

Figure 3.3: Binary entropy function, $H(p) = -p \log p - (1 - p) \log(1 - p)$, using base 2 logarithm.

Another way of looking at $H(p)$ is in terms of information. Imagine that winning a bet is represented by the symbol 1 and losing by the symbol 0. A long series of games would then be represented by a long string of ones and zeros. If the probability of winning is $p = 1$ then the string would be composed of nothing but ones which is rather boring and conveys no information. Likewise for $p = 0$ the string would be all zeros, also no information. In both these cases $H(p) = 0$.

For $p = \frac{1}{2}$ there would be a similar number of ones and zeros in the string, meaning that it conveys the maximum amount of information. Each position in the string provides information about the outcome of a game that has a maximum uncertainty. Data compression techniques will have little effect on reducing the length of the string so that a minimum of 1 bit is required to represent each position in the string. Note that in this case $H(\frac{1}{2}) = 1$. $H(p)$ is a measure of the average number of bits required to encode the symbols in the string.

In the base 2 logarithm eq.3.28 becomes

$$G = 1 - H(p) \qquad (3.30)$$

When winning is certain $p = 1, f = 1, H(1) = 0$, and $G = 1$. This is the case discussed previously where you bet your entire bankroll and it doubles every time, $a_n = 2^n$. When $p = \frac{1}{2}, f = 0, H(\frac{1}{2}) = 1$, and $G = 0$, the Kelly system says to bet nothing in this case since in the long run you will get nowhwere. For $\frac{1}{2} < p < 1$ you get $0 < G < 1$ and you can expect exponential growth of your bankroll in the long run.

Of course expectation does not tell the whole story. You need to look at variance too. To calculate the variance, start with eq.3.1 which is repeated below

$$a_{n+1} = (1 + x_n f)a_n \qquad (3.31)$$

Taking the logarithm of this equation gives

$$\log a_{n+1} = \log a_n + \log(1 + x_n f) \qquad (3.32)$$

Now taking the variance gives

$$\text{Var}[\log a_{n+1}] = \text{Var}[\log a_n] + \text{Var}[\log(1 + x_n f)] \qquad (3.33)$$

This difference equation for the variance can easily be solved once the variance of $\log(1 + x_n f)$ has been found. That variance is

$$\text{Var}[\log(1 + x_n f)] = E[\log^2(1 + x_n f)] \qquad (3.34)$$
$$- E^2[\log(1 + x_n f)]$$

and the expectations are

$$E[\log(1 + x_n f)] = p \log(1 + f) + (1 - p) \log(1 - f) \qquad (3.35)$$

$$E[\log^2(1+x_nf)] = p\log^2(1+f)+(1-p)\log^2(1-f) \quad (3.36)$$

Substituting these into eq.3.34 and simplifying gives

$$\text{Var}[\log(1+x_nf)] = p(1-p)\log^2\left(\frac{1+f}{1-f}\right) \quad (3.37)$$

Now since $\text{Var}[\log a_0] = 0$, eq.3.33 becomes

$$\text{Var}[\log a_n] = np(1-p)\log^2\left(\frac{1+f}{1-f}\right) \quad (3.38)$$

For a fixed n and p the variance changes as a function of f by the factor

$$\log^2\left(\frac{1+f}{1-f}\right) \quad (3.39)$$

A plot of this is shown in figure 3.4. For small f this is a slowly increasing function but for f close to 1, the increase is rapid as you would expect. Now if you substitute in the optimal value of f given by eq.3.26 then the variance is

$$\text{Var}[\log a_n] = np(1-p)\log^2\left(\frac{p}{1-p}\right) \quad (3.40)$$

A plot of this for fixed n is shown in figure 3.5. This is an interesting plot. It shows that the variance increases as p

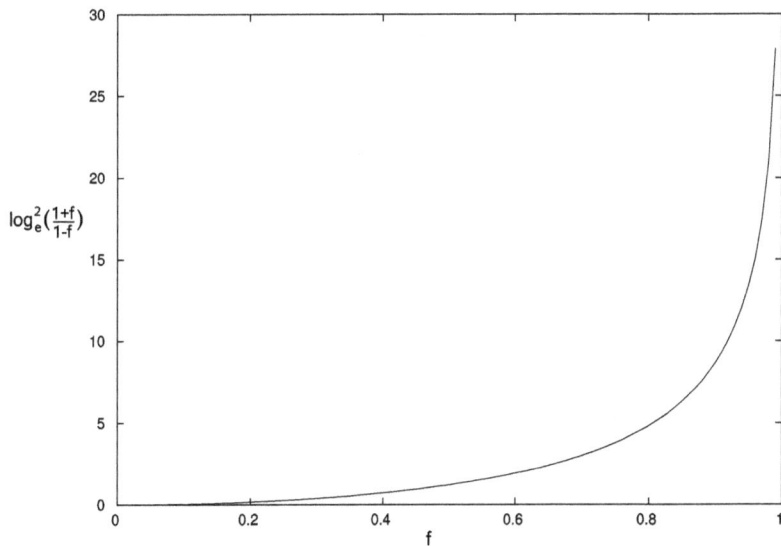

Figure 3.4: For a fixed n and p, the variance of the bankroll, a_n, changes according to this function, $\log^2\left(\frac{1+f}{1-f}\right)$. The logarithm is base e here.

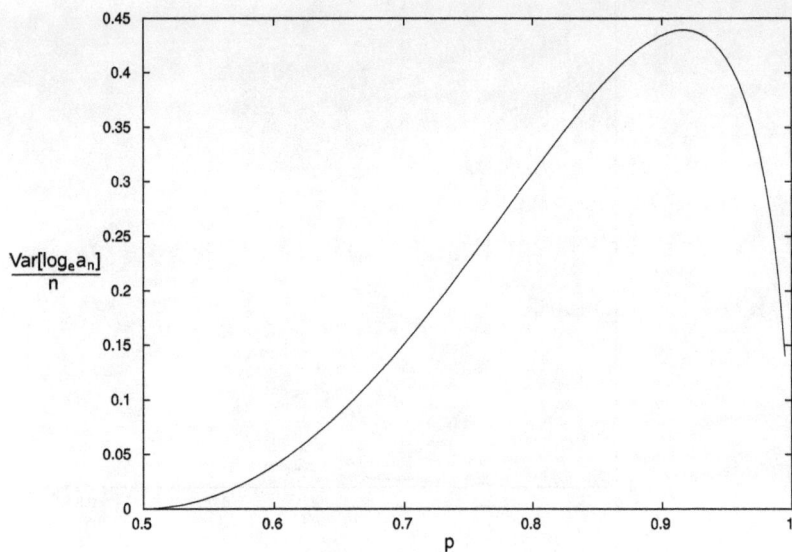

Figure 3.5: Variance of the logarithm (base e) of the bankroll, a_n, for fixed n.

increases until it reaches a maxium and then rapidly goes to zero as p approaches 1. The value of p at the maximum satisfies the equation

$$\log\left(\frac{p}{1-p}\right) = \frac{2}{2p-1} \qquad (3.41)$$

The value is approximately $p = 0.91678$. The plot shows that there is an interesting trade off between f and p. For small p, f will be small so that even though there is a small probability of winning, the size of your bankroll will not fluctuate much on average. As p increases so does f so that bankroll fluctuations become larger. At some point however, the probability of winning becomes so great that the variance begins to decrease rapidly. There is a caveat here that you should keep in mind however. When p is close to 1, you will be betting most of your bankroll so that a loss, although unlikely, could be devastating.

3.4   Bankroll Probabilities

To get a clearer picture of the Kelly system in operation let's look at the probability that the bankroll, a_n, is above or below some value A. What is the probability for example that a_n will be at least double the initial bankroll or that it will be less than half the initial bankroll. You would expect that the probability of at least doubling goes to 1 for large n and the probability of being less than half goes to 0. Using eq.3.7 for a_n, the condition $a_n \geq A$ is

$$(1+f)^k(1-f)^{n-k} \geq A \qquad (3.42)$$

which is equivalent to

$$k \geq \frac{\log A - n\log(1-f)}{\log(1+f) - \log(1-f)} = B \qquad (3.43)$$

The probability that $a_n \geq A$ is equal to the probability that the number of wins k, is greater than or equal to B.

Recall that there are $\binom{n}{k}$ ways of having k wins in n bets and each of these ways has a probability of $p^k(1-p)^{n-k}$ therefore

$$P(k \geq B) = \sum_{k=\lceil B \rceil}^{n} \binom{n}{k} p^k(1-p)^{n-k} \qquad (3.44)$$

where $\lceil B \rceil$ means the smallest integer that is greater than or equal to B. Instead of using this equation it is more convenient to use the normal approximation to the binomial distribution which gives

$$P(k \geq B) \approx \frac{1}{\sqrt{2\pi npq}} \int_{B}^{\infty} \exp\left(\frac{-(k-np)^2}{2npq}\right) dk \qquad (3.45)$$

Figure 3.6 shows the probability that $a_n \geq 2$ for $p = 0.6$ and $f = 2p - 1 = 0.2$. You can see that the probability of at least doubling your money after 100 bets is about

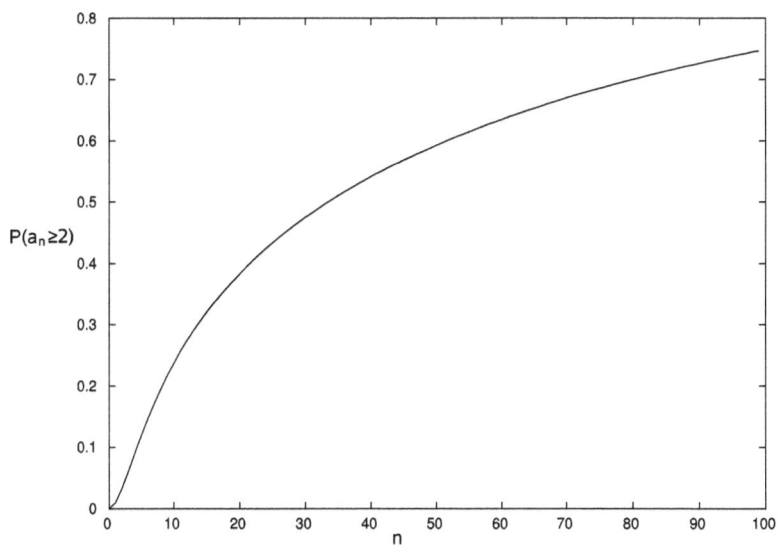

Figure 3.6: Probability that the bankroll $a_n \geq 2$ for $p = 0.6$ and $f = 2p - 1 = 0.2$.

0.75. Likewise the probability that $a_n \leq A$ is equal to the probability that $k \leq B$ which you can also express as $P(k \leq B) = 1 - P(k > B)$, or using the normal approximation

$$P(k \leq B) \approx \frac{1}{\sqrt{2\pi npq}} \int_{-\infty}^{B} \exp\left(\frac{-(k - np)^2}{2npq}\right) dk \quad (3.46)$$

3.5   Multiple Simultaneous Games

3.5.1   Two Games

Now we look at the situation where multiple games are played simultaneously. First consider the case of just two bets. Let b_n be the amount bet on game 1 and c_n be the amount bet on game 2, then the bankroll obeys the following equation

$$a_{n+1} = a_n + x_n b_n + y_n c_n \quad (3.47)$$

where x_n and y_n are random variables that take on the values +1 and -1 corresponding to winning or losing the game. The probabilities for x_n and y_n will be discussed later. For fixed fraction betting let f_1 be the bankroll fraction bet on game 1 and f_2 be the fraction bet on game 2, then $b_n = f_1 a_n$, $c_n = f_2 a_n$, and eq.3.47 becomes

$$a_{n+1} = a_n(1 + x_n f_1 + y_n f_2) \quad (3.48)$$

Iterating this equation gives the following equation for a_n

$$a_n = a_0 \prod_{k=0}^{n-1} (1 + x_k f_1 + y_k f_2) \qquad (3.49)$$

Once again, from here on assume that the initial bankroll is $a_0 = 1$.

The bankroll expectation is

$$E[a_n] = \prod_{k=0}^{n-1} E[1 + x_k f_1 + y_k f_2] \qquad (3.50)$$

where the expectation of the product terms are all identical and equal to

$$
\begin{aligned}
E[1 + x_k f_1 + y_k f_2] = \ & (1 + f_1 + f_2) p_{++} \qquad (3.51) \\
& + (1 + f_1 - f_1) p_{+-} \\
& + (1 - f_1 + f_2) p_{-+} \\
& + (1 - f_1 - f_2) p_{--}
\end{aligned}
$$

where $p_{++} = P(x_k = +1, y_k = +1)$ and so on. Substituting this into eq.3.50 and collecting terms gives

$$
\begin{aligned}
E[a_n] = \ & (1 + (p_{++} + p_{+-} - p_{-+} - p_{--}) f_1 \\
& + (p_{++} - p_{+-} + p_{-+} - p_{---}) f_2)^n
\end{aligned} \qquad (3.52)
$$

Now consider the case where the two games are independent so that the joint probabilities are equal to the product of the individual probabilities

$$
\begin{aligned}
p_{++} &= P(x_k = +1)P(y_k = +1) = p_1 p_2 \quad (3.53) \\
p_{+-} &= p_1(1 - p_2) = p_1 q_2 \\
p_{-+} &= (1 - p_1)p_2 = q_1 p_2 \\
p_{--} &= (1 - p_1)(1 - p_2) = q_1 q_2
\end{aligned}
$$

Substituting these probabilities into eq.3.51 and simplifying gives

$$
\begin{aligned}
E[1 + x_k f_1 + y_k f_2] &= 1 + (2p_1 - 1)f_1 \quad (3.54) \\
&\quad + (2p_2 - 1)f_2
\end{aligned}
$$

The bankroll expectation is then

$$
E[a_n] = (1 + (2p_1 - 1)f_1 + (2p_2 - 1)f_2)^n \quad (3.55)
$$

Trying to maximize either eq.3.52 or eq.3.55 with respect to f_1 and f_2 would simply lead to the conclusion that these fractions should be as large as possible.

We will instead use the Kelly criterion and maximize the expectation of $\log a_n$ but first we will look at the variance of a_n. To calculate the variance, first write a_n in the following form

$$a_n = (1 + f_1 + f_2)^j (1 + f_1 - f_2)^k (1 - f_1 + f_2)^l (1 - f_1 - f_2)^m$$
$$(3.56)$$

where $j + k + l + m = n$.

For the variance, we need $E[a_n^2]$ which, using eq.3.56, can be expressed as

$$E[a_n^2] = \sum_{j+k+l+m=n} \left((1 + f_1 + f_2)^2 p_{++}\right)^j \left((1 + f_1 - f_2)^2 p_{+-}\right)^k \cdot$$
$$\left((1 - f_1 + f_2)^2 p_{-+}\right)^l \left((1 - f_1 - f_2)^2 p_{--}\right)^m \binom{n}{j\ k\ l\ m}$$
$$(3.57)$$

where

$$\binom{n}{j\ k\ l\ m} = \frac{n!}{j!\ k!\ l!\ m!} \qquad (3.58)$$

is a multinomial coefficient. Eq.3.57 is a multinomial expansion that is equal to

$$E[a_n^2] = ((1 + f_1 + f_2)^2 p_{++} + (1 + f_1 - f_2)^2 p_{+-}$$
$$+ (1 - f_1 + f_2)^2 p_{-+} + (1 - f_1 - f_2)^2 p_{--})^n \qquad (3.59)$$

To get the expression for the case of independent games, use the substitutions in eq.3.53. The variance is then simply calculated as

$$\text{Var}[a_n^2] = E[a_n^2] - E^2[a_n] \qquad (3.60)$$

Now on to the Kelly criterion. We will do the analysis only for the case of independent games. The dependent game analysis is similar. First we need the expectation of $\log a_n$

$$E[\log a_n] = \sum_{k=0}^{n-1} E[\log(1 + x_k f_1 + y_k f_2)] \qquad (3.61)$$

where the expectation of the sum terms is

$$\begin{aligned}
E[\log(1 + x_k f_1 + y_k f_2)] &= p_1 p_2 \log(1 + f_1 + f_2) \\
&+ p_1 q_2 \log(1 + f_1 - f_2) \\
&+ q_1 p_2 \log(1 - f_1 + f_2) \\
&+ q_1 q_2 \log(1 - f_1 - f_2)
\end{aligned} \qquad (3.62)$$

This is independent of k so the sum in eq.3.61 is just n times this. Eq.3.62 is in fact the long term exponential growth rate that we want to maximize

$$\begin{aligned}
G = \frac{1}{n} E[\log a_n] &= p_1 p_2 \log(1 + f_1 + f_2) \\
&+ p_1 q_2 \log(1 + f_1 - f_2) \\
&+ q_1 p_2 \log(1 - f_1 + f_2) \\
&+ q_1 q_2 \log(1 - f_1 - f_2)
\end{aligned} \qquad (3.63)$$

To maximize this with respect to f_1 and f_2 you take the partial derivatives of G with respect to f_1 and f_2, set them equal to zero and solve for f_1 and f_2. The two equations to solve are

$$\frac{\partial G}{\partial f_1} = \frac{p_1 p_2}{1 + f_1 + f_2} + \frac{p_1 q_2}{1 + f_1 - f_2}$$
$$- \frac{q_1 p_2}{1 - f_1 + f_2} - \frac{q_1 q_2}{1 - f_1 - f_2} = 0 \qquad (3.64)$$

$$\frac{\partial G}{\partial f_2} = \frac{p_1 p_2}{1 + f_1 + f_2} - \frac{p_1 q_2}{1 + f_1 - f_2}$$
$$+ \frac{q_1 p_2}{1 - f_1 + f_2} - \frac{q_1 q_2}{1 - f_1 - f_2} = 0 \qquad (3.65)$$

These equations simplify to

$$f_1 + f_2 = \frac{p_1 p_2 - q_1 q_2}{p_1 p_2 + q_1 q_2} = d \qquad (3.66)$$

$$f_1 - f_2 = \frac{p_1 q_2 - q_1 p_2}{p_1 q_2 + q_1 p_2} = e \qquad (3.67)$$

so that f_1 and f_2 are equal to

$$f_1 = \frac{d + e}{2} \qquad (3.68)$$

$$f_2 = \frac{d - e}{2} \qquad (3.69)$$

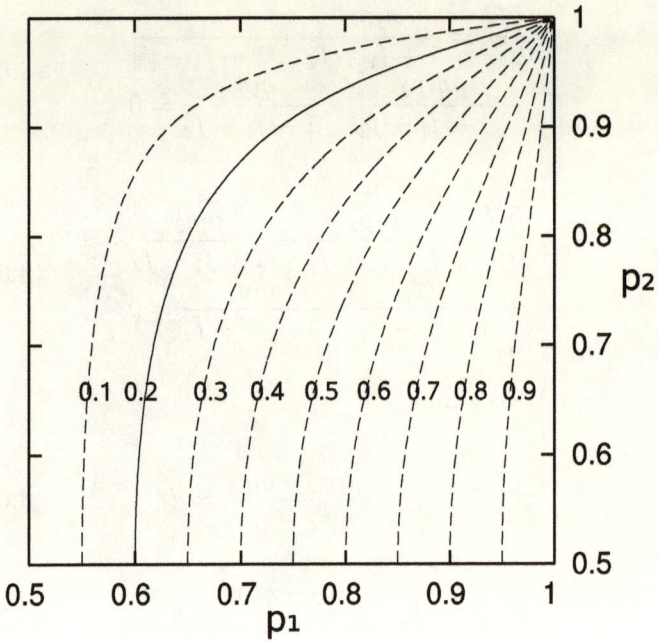

Figure 3.7: Contour plot for f_1.

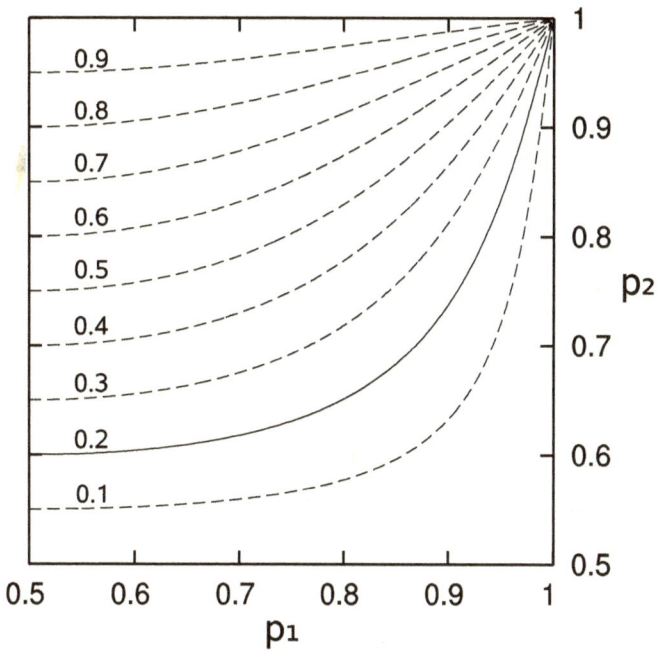

Figure 3.8: Contour plot for f_2.

Contour plots for f_1 and f_2 are shown in figures 3.7 and 3.8. Substituting these expressions for f_1 and f_2 into equation 3.62 for G and simplifying gives

$$G(p_1, p_2) = 1 - H(p_1) - H(p_2) + I(p_1, p_2) \qquad (3.70)$$

where $H(p_i)$ is the usual binary entropy function

$$H(p_i) = -p_i \log p_i - (1 - p_i) \log(1 - p_i) \qquad (3.71)$$

and the function $I(p_1, p_2)$ is given by

$$
\begin{aligned}
I(p_1, p_2) = &-(p_1 p_2 + q_1 q_2) \log(p_1 p_2 + q_1 q_2) \\
&-(p_1 q_2 + q_1 p_2) \log(p_1 q_2 + q_1 p_2)
\end{aligned}
\qquad (3.72)
$$

This is also a binary entropy function which you can see by defining the variables

$$
\begin{aligned}
p &= p_1 p_2 + q_1 q_2 = \frac{1 + (2p_1 - 1)(2p_2 - 1)}{2} & (3.73) \\
q &= p_1 q_2 + q_1 p_2 = \frac{1 - (2p_1 - 1)(2p_2 - 1)}{2} & (3.74) \\
&= 1 - p
\end{aligned}
$$

A contour plot for G is shown in figure 3.9. Now let's look at the case where both games have the same probabilities.

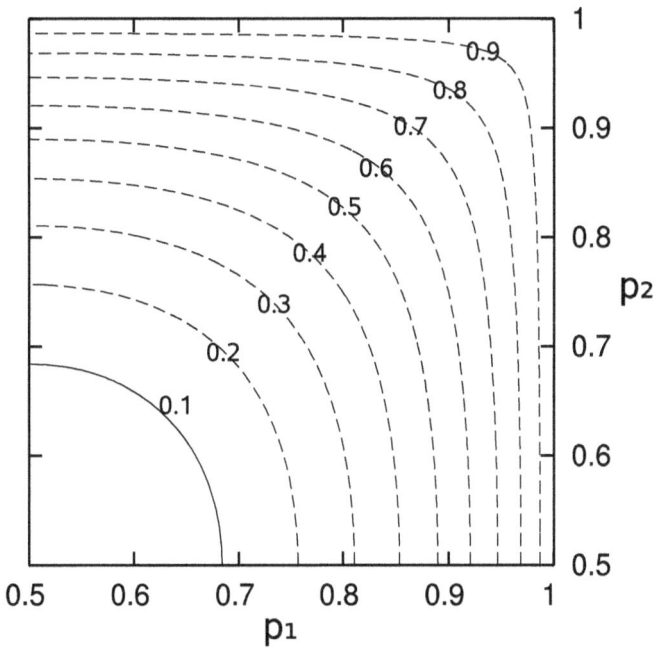

Figure 3.9: Contour plot for long term exponential growth rate, $G(p_1, p_2) = 1 - H(p_1) - H(p_2) + I(p_1, p_2)$.

Let $p_1 = p_2 = p$, then the betting fractions must be equal and from eq.3.66 we have

$$f = \frac{2p - 1}{2(1 - 2pq)} \qquad (3.75)$$

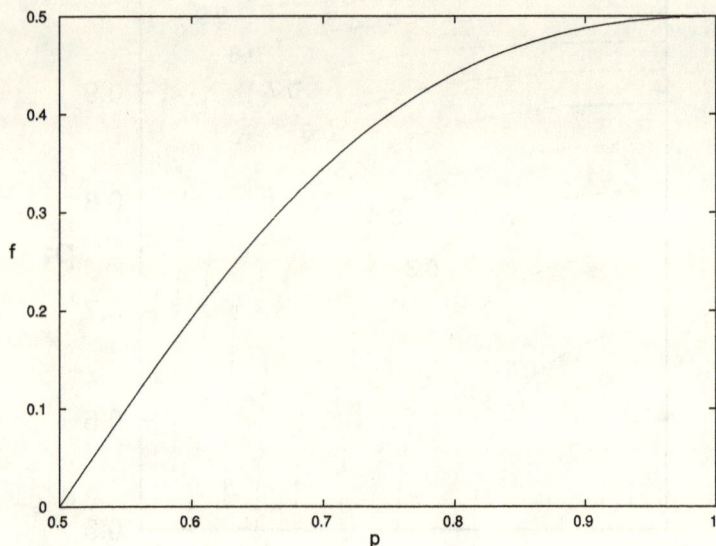

Figure 3.10: Kelly fraction for two games with same probabilities, $f = \frac{2p-1}{2(1-2pq)}$.

A plot of this is shown in figure 3.10. The expression for G in this case simplifies to

$$G(p) = 1 - 2H(p) + I(p) \qquad (3.76)$$

where $H(p)$ is the usual binary entropy function and $I(p)$

is given by

$$I(p) = -(1 - 2pq)\log(1 - 2pq) - 2pq\log(2pq) \qquad (3.77)$$

A plot of $G(p)$ is shown in figure 3.11 along with a plot of $G(p)$ for a single game, for comparison.

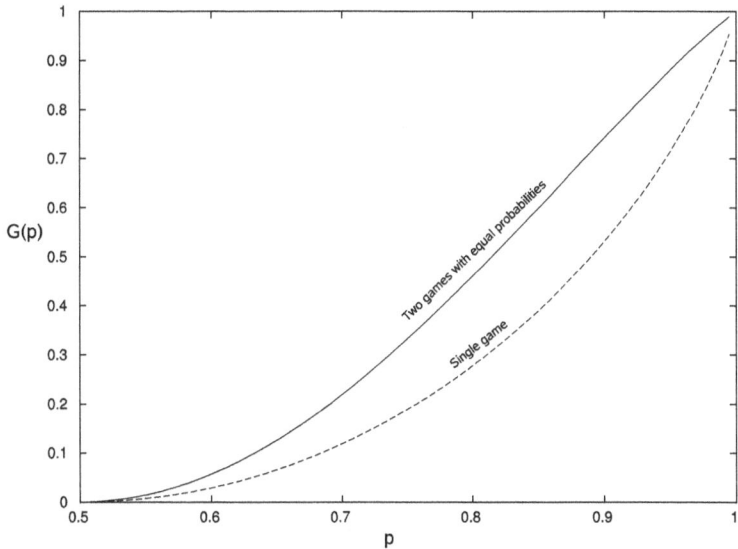

Figure 3.11: Long term exponential growth rate for two games with equal probabilities $G(p) = 1 - 2H(p) + I(p)$, and a single game $G(p) = 1 - H(p)$.

3.5.2   Three Games

We will now outline the solution for three games. The expectation of $\log a_n$ in this case is

$$E[\log a_n] = \sum_{k=0}^{n-1} E[\log(1 + x_k f_1 + y_k f_2 + z_k f_3)] \quad (3.78)$$

where x_k, y_k, and z_k are once again random variables that can take on the values +1 or -1 corresponding to the win or loss of a game. The possible ways in which the fractions can combine is

$$a = f_1 + f_2 + f_3 \quad (3.79)$$
$$b = f_1 + f_2 - f_3$$
$$c = f_1 - f_2 + f_3$$
$$d = f_1 - f_2 - f_3$$

plus the negative of these terms. Note that these combinations are not independent since

$$a + d = b + c \quad (3.80)$$

In terms of these combinations the exponential growth term can be written as

$$
\begin{aligned}
G &= E[\log(1 + x_k f_1 + y_k f_2 + z_k f_3)] \qquad (3.81)\\
&= p_1 p_2 p_3 \log(1 + a) + q_1 q_2 q_3 \log(1 - a) +\\
&\quad p_1 p_2 q_3 \log(1 + b) + q_1 q_2 p_3 \log(1 - b) +\\
&\quad p_1 q_2 p_3 \log(1 + c) + q_1 p_2 q_3 \log(1 - c) +\\
&\quad q_1 p_2 p_3 \log(1 + d) + p_1 q_2 q_3 \log(1 - d)
\end{aligned}
$$

Now G can be maximized with respect to the variables a, b, c, and d subject to the constraint of eq.3.80. The maximum is found by solving the equations

$$
\begin{aligned}
\frac{\partial G}{\partial a} &= \lambda \qquad (3.82)\\
\frac{\partial G}{\partial b} &= -\lambda\\
\frac{\partial G}{\partial c} &= -\lambda\\
\frac{\partial G}{\partial d} &= \lambda\\
a + d &= b + c
\end{aligned}
$$

There are 5 equations here with 5 unknowns a, b, c, d, e, and λ. Substituting the derivatives, the equations are

$$
\begin{aligned}
p_1p_2p_3 - q_1q_2q_3 - a(p_1p_2p_3 + q_1q_2q_3) &= \lambda(1 - a^2) \\
p_1p_2q_3 - q_1q_2p_3 - b(p_1p_2q_3 + q_1q_2p_3) &= -\lambda(1 - b^2) \\
p_1q_2p_3 - q_1p_2q_3 - c(p_1q_2p_3 + q_1p_2q_3) &= -\lambda(1 - c^2) \\
q_1p_2p_3 - p_1q_2q_3 - d(q_1p_2p_3 + p_1q_2q_3) &= \lambda(1 - d^2) \\
a + d &= b + c \quad (3.83)
\end{aligned}
$$

These equations will generally have to be solved numerically. Once solved, the betting fractions are calculated as follows:

$$
f_1 = \frac{a + d}{2} \qquad f_2 = \frac{a - c}{2} \qquad f_3 = \frac{a - b}{2} \qquad (3.84)
$$

The same basic procedure can be used for more than 3 games but things become very complicated for a large number of games.

3.5.3   Identical Games

The problem becomes much simpler when all the games have the same probability of winning. In this case all the betting fractions must be equal and the bankroll equation is

$$
a_n = \prod_{k=0}^{n-1} (1 + x_k f) \qquad (3.85)
$$

For N identical games, the random variable x_k can take on $N + 1$ values. If the number of games that win is $W = 0, 1, 2, \ldots N$, then the possible values of x_k are given by

$$x_k = 2W - N \tag{3.86}$$
$$= -N, -N+2, \ldots, N-2, N \tag{3.87}$$

and the probabilities are

$$P(x_k = 2W - N) = \binom{N}{W} p^W (1 - p)^{N-W} \tag{3.88}$$

where p is the probability that any one of the games wins. The expectation of a_n is

$$E[a_n] = \prod_{k=0}^{n-1} E[1 + x_k f] \tag{3.89}$$

where

$$E[1 + x_k f] = 1 + f E[x_k] \tag{3.90}$$

To get the variance of a_n we will also need the expectation of x_k^2. In general the expectation of the nth power of x_k is given by

$$E[x_k^n] = \sum_{W=0}^{N} (2W - N)^n \binom{N}{W} p^W (1-p)^{N-W} \qquad (3.91)$$

These moments can best be calculated with the moment generating function. The moment generating function for x_k is the same as the one derived in eq.2.17

$$M_{x_k}(s) = (pe^s + qe^{-s})^N \qquad (3.92)$$

The two moments we need are then

$$E[x_k] = \left. \frac{dM_{x_k}(s)}{ds} \right|_{s=0} = N(2p - 1) \qquad (3.93)$$

$$E[x_k^2] = \left. \frac{d^2 M_{x_k}(s)}{ds^2} \right|_{s=0} = N(N - 1)(2p - 1)^2 + N \qquad (3.94)$$

The expectation of a_n is then

$$E[a_n] = (1 + N(2p - 1)f)^n \qquad (3.95)$$

and the expectation of a_n^2 is

$$E[a_n^2] = \prod_{k=0}^{n-1} E[(1 + x_k f)^2] \qquad (3.96)$$

where

$$
\begin{aligned}
E[(1 + x_k f)^2] &= E[1 + 2x_k f + x_k^2 f^2] \quad\quad (3.97)\\
&= 1 + 2f E[x_k] + f^2 E[x_k^2]\\
&= (1 + N(2p - 1)f)^2 + 4Npqf^2
\end{aligned}
$$

The variance of a_n is then given by

$$
\begin{aligned}
\mathrm{Var}[a_n] &= E[a_n^2] - E^2[a_n] \quad\quad (3.98)\\
&= ((1 + N(2p - 1)f)^2 + 4Npqf^2)^n\\
&\quad - (1 + N(2p - 1)f)^{2n}
\end{aligned}
$$

An interesting thing to note is what happens when you let $f = \frac{1}{N}$. In this case the entire bankroll is bet, distributed evenly among all the games, and the expectation becomes

$$
E[a_n] = (2p)^n \quad\quad (3.99)
$$

This is the same expectation as betting the entire bankroll on a single game with probability p of winning. The variance in this case is however different. With $f = \frac{1}{N}$ the variance for the N games is

$$
\mathrm{Var}[a_n] = \left((2p)^2 + \frac{4pq}{N}\right)^n - (2p)^{2n} \quad\quad (3.100)
$$

Note that the variance goes to zero as N goes to infinity for the case of finite n. In contrast the single game variance for $f = 1$ is

$$\text{Var}[a_n] = (4p)^n - (2p)^{2n} \tag{3.101}$$

Now we apply the Kelly criterion to this case.

The expectation of $\log a_n$ is

$$E[\log a_n] = \sum_{k=0}^{n-1} E[\log(1 + x_k f)] = nG \tag{3.102}$$

The exponential growth rate is equal to the expectation of the sum terms

$$
\begin{aligned}
G &= E[\log(1 + x_k f)] &\tag{3.103} \\
&= \sum_{W=0}^{N} \binom{N}{W} p^W (1 - p)^{N-W} \log(1 + (2W - N)f)
\end{aligned}
$$

As usual, to maximize this, you set the derivative of G with respect to f equal to zero and solve for f. This is easy to do for $N = 2$ but for larger N it is best to use root finding software. We will look at the example of $N = 3$. In this case G is

$$G = q^3 \log(1 - 3f) + 3pq^2 \log(1 - f)$$
$$+ 3p^2 q(1 + f) + p^3 \log(1 + 3f) \tag{3.104}$$

and we want to solve

$$\frac{dG}{df} = -\frac{3q^3}{1 - 3f} - \frac{3pq^2}{1 - f} + \frac{3p^2 q}{1 + f} + \frac{3p^3}{1 + 3f} = 0 \tag{3.105}$$

This equation simplifies to

$$3(4pq + (2p - 1)^2)f^3 - (8pq + 1)(2p - 1)f^2$$
$$- (4pq + 3(2p - 1)^2)f + (2p - 1) = 0 \tag{3.106}$$

The problem then is to find the roots of a third degree polynomial in f. This is best done using root finding software.

3.6 Kelly Plays Powerball

Powerball is a lottery run by the Multi-State Lottery Association (MUSL) which is made up of 31 states and the District of Columbia. MUSL is a non-profit organization which means that excess proceeds from the lottery are distributed to the association members. It is unclear what percentage of the proceeds is used for prize money but it is almost certainly less than 50 percent.

Lotteries are almost never a good bet. The odds of winning are usually very low but people are attracted to them because of the large prizes that can be won. In the case of Powerball, the grandprize can reach into the hundreds of millions of dollars. There is no rational way to justify playing a game with such bad odds but then few people view gambling as a rational pursuit. In a perfectly rational world there would be no casinos and less fun and excitement.

The one dollar that it costs to buy a single Powerball ticket has less utility to most people than the chance it brings, however small, of winning a prize in the millions of dollars. There is nothing irrational about this, up to a point. There is no shortage of stories (true or not) about people spending their last dollar on a Powerball ticket and becoming millionaires.

How much net worth should one have in order to justify the purchase of a $1 Powerball ticket? There is really no objective way to answer this question, since people have different utility functions for their money. The Kelly criterion does offer one way to calculate the required net worth for playing Powerball. The calculation is performed below, but you can see that it really makes no sense in this case. If people played Powerball using the Kelly criterion, then very few tickets would be sold, and the lottery would soon go out of business.

Is it possible to turn Powerball from a gamble into an investment? At first this sounds like an absurd question. We will show below, however, that when the grand prize becomes large enough, the expected return from playing Powerball becomes positive. At first glance therefore, it meets one of the conditions for being an investment, i.e. a positive expected return. For something to be considered an investment, however, the positive returns must be realized in a reasonable amount of time. Playing Powerball does not come anywhere close to meeting this condition. On average, the game would have to be played at very high grand prize levels for thousands of years before the positive expected returns could be realized. Powerball is a perfect illustration of the fact that a positive expected return is not enough. You also need to be able to realize the return in a reasonable amount of time.

We will start our Powerball analysis by describing the mechanics of how the game is played. In a Powerball drawing, 5 numbers are chosen from the numbers 1 through 55, and then there is a separate drawing of one number from the numbers 1 through 42. This last single number is called the Powerball number. The actual process of drawing the numbers involves randomly choosing 5 white balls from a drum of 55 white balls marked with the numbers 1 through 55. The Powerball number is gotten by randomly choosing 1 red ball from a separate drum of 42 red balls marked with the numbers 1 through 42.

You play the game by purchasing a ticket with 5 numbers chosen from 1 through 55, and a Powerball number chosen from 1 through 42. There can be no duplicates in the 5 numbers that you choose. You can either choose the numbers yourself, or you can have a computer randomly choose the numbers for you when you purchase the ticket. The cost of a single ticket is $1. The prizes are awarded based upon how many of the 5 numbers you match with the drawing, and whether or not you match the Powerball number. The value of the grand prize is determined by how many tickets are sold, while the values of the lesser prizes are fixed. For an extra $1 you have the option of multiplying the lesser prizes by a randomly chosen factor of 2 through 5. This is called the powerplay option.

The table below shows the prizes associated with the different ways of matching the numbers in the drawing. The *wb* column refers to how many of the 5 white ball numbers are matched, and the *pb* column refers to whether or not the Powerball is matched, with 1 meaning a match, and 0 no match. Note that not all possible ways of matching are awarded a prize.

To calculate the probabilities of winning each of the prizes, you have to determine how many ways the matches can be made, and also how many unique possible tickets there are. You also have to keep in mind that the order of the numbers in the drawing and on the tickets is irrelevant. In other words, a permutation of the 5 numbers in the drawing or on the ticket does not count as a different set of numbers. The total number of ways of choosing 5 numbers from the set of numbers 1 through 55 is equal to

$$\frac{55 \cdot 54 \cdot 53 \cdot 52 \cdot 51}{5 \cdot 4 \cdot 3 \cdot 2 \cdot 1} = \binom{55}{5} \qquad (3.107)$$

wb	pb	Prize $
0	0	0
0	1	3
1	0	0
1	1	4
2	0	0
2	1	7
3	0	7
3	1	100
4	0	100
4	1	10000
5	0	200000
5	1	Grand Prize

Table 3.1: Matches associated with prizes in Powerball.

where we have used the binomial coefficient notation defined as

$$\binom{n}{k} = \frac{n!}{k!(n-k)!} \tag{3.108}$$

The number of ways of choosing the Powerball from the numbers 1 through 42 is just 42. The total number of possible unique tickets is then

$$\text{Unique tickets} = 42\binom{55}{5} = 146,107,962 \tag{3.109}$$

Now the number of ways of matching exactly n of the 5 white balls in a drawing is given by

$$N(wb = n) = \binom{5}{n}\binom{50}{5-n} \qquad (3.110)$$

so that the probability of matching exactly n white balls

$$P(wb = n) = \frac{\binom{5}{n}\binom{50}{5-n}}{\binom{55}{5}} \qquad (3.111)$$

where $n = 0, 1, \ldots, 5$. The probability of matching the Powerball is

$$P(pb = 1) = \frac{1}{42} \qquad (3.112)$$

and the probability of not matching the Powerball is

$$P(pb = 0) = \frac{41}{42} \qquad (3.113)$$

The following table lists all the possible outcomes of a drawing along with their probabilities, and odds.

The overall chance of winning 1 of the 9 prizes is equal to

$$P(win) = \frac{10559}{386529} = \frac{1}{36.6066} \qquad (3.114)$$

and the overall chance of not winning anything is

$$P(lose) = \frac{375970}{386529} = \frac{1}{1.0281} \qquad (3.115)$$

wb	pb	Probability	Odds 1 in
0	0	$\frac{6204940}{10436283}$	1.6819
0	1	$\frac{151340}{10436283}$	68.9592
1	0	$\frac{3372250}{10436283}$	3.0948
1	1	$\frac{82250}{10436283}$	126.8849
2	0	$\frac{574000}{10436283}$	18.1817
2	1	$\frac{14000}{10436283}$	745.4488
3	0	$\frac{35875}{10436283}$	290.9068
3	1	$\frac{875}{10436283}$	11927.1806
4	0	$\frac{5125}{73053981}$	14254.4353
4	1	$\frac{125}{73053981}$	584431.8480
5	0	$\frac{41}{146107962}$	3563608.8293
5	1	$\frac{1}{146107962}$	146107962.0000

Table 3.2: Probabilities and odds associated with winning matches in Powerball.

Let us imagine now that exactly 1 of every possible Powerball ticket was sold. The total proceeds from the ticket sales would be $146,107,962. How large can the grand prize be for the lottery just to break even? The total amount of money the lottery would have to pay out in this case is $28,800,030 + GP$. Setting this equal to the total ticket sales, and solving for GP gives a maximum grand prize of $GP = \$117,307,932$. It turns out that this is also the value of the grand prize, above which, the expected return becomes positive. Of course since probably no more than 50% of ticket sales revenue goes towards prizes, the grand prize in this case would be much less.

Calculating the expected return, using the probabilities and prize values, gives us the following function

$$\frac{GP - 1}{146107962} - \frac{9023687}{11239074} \tag{3.116}$$

The expectation is zero when the grand prize is equal to $117,307,932. When the grand prize is below this value, you will lose money in the long run. When it is above this value, you will make money in the long run. You have to be careful about the term 'long run' here. What it means is that you would have to play the game for thousands of years with the jackpot being greater than 117 million each time in order to realize a positive expected return.

Now let's look at what the Kelly criterion has to say about playing Powerball and one's net worth. The Kelly fraction for any gamble or investment is the largest fraction of one's assets that can be put into play without risking ruin. If you calculate the Kelly fraction for Powerball, then assuming only one ticket is purchased for $1, the required net worth to play the game according to the Kelly criterion would be one over the fraction. Figure 3.12 shows the required net worth as a function of the grand prize. Note that at a grandprize value of $117,307,932 the minimum worth is ∞ because the expectation is zero. The Kelly criterion is very misleading in this case however. Since the time scale for realizing expectations is so long, and net worth tends to grow with time from other sources, there is no chance of ruin from playing $1 Powerball games unless one's net worth is extremely small.

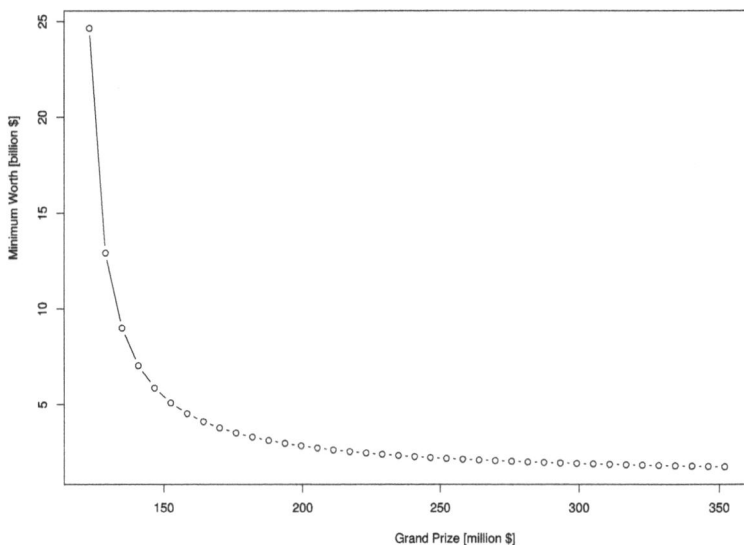

Figure 3.12: Minimum Worth [billion $] vs. Grand Prize [million $].

This page intentionally left blank.

Chapter 4

Investing with Kelly

There is no fundamental difference between investing and gambling. An investment is always a gamble, which is to say that positive returns are never 100% certain. There are so called risk free investments in which the probability of loss becomes negligible but the returns are correspondingly very small. A three month U.S. Treasury bill is a good example. The probability of default is extremely small (although not zero) but the return can go below 1%. Contrast this with the stock market where positive returns can be very high - over 100% is not unheard of. The possibility of a negative return, or loss, however is by no means negligible in the stock market. A higher expected return is almost always accompanied by higher return volatility as measured by the variance or standard deviation of the returns. If you had to distinguish investing from gambling you could say that investing usually has a higher expected return for a given amount of volatility. The exact value of this ratio that marks the border between investing and gambling is a matter of taste. Another distinguishing feature of investments is that the probability of total loss of the investment is usually small.

In discussing the use of the Kelly method, we will use the stock market as the model investment. We will start by looking at investment in a single stock. Next we look at how the inclusion of a risk free investment changes things. Finally we will look at investing in more than one stock at a time.

4.1   Single Stock Investment

Let's start by defining what we mean by the return on a stock. First we have to define a time interval over which the return will be measured. Stock prices change almost continuously during the course of a trading day. Let $S(t)$ represent the price of a stock at time t then the return on the stock at time t for a time interval T is

$$r(t) = \frac{s(t) - s(t-T)}{s(t-T)} = \frac{s(t)}{s(t-T)} - 1 \quad (4.1)$$
$$= R(t) - 1$$

The term $R(t) = s(t)/s(t-T)$ is sometimes called the total return and $r(t)$ is called the rate of return. We will just refer to $r(t)$ as the return. The time interval T can be 1 hour, 1 day, or 1 year, as long as it is constant.

It is evident from eq.4.1 that there are an unlimited number of possible return values. However for computational purposes the number of return values will have to be limited to a finite set. How do you determine which set of values to use? The simplest method is to produce a histogram of the returns from historical stock price data. Start by picking a time interval T then calculate returns using eq.4.1 starting at some time t.

You will end up with a set of returns that has a maximum value, r_{max}, and a minimum value, r_{min}. Now decide how many return values you want to use. If N is the number of values, then the size of the histogram bins will be

$$\Delta = \frac{r_{max} - r_{min}}{N} \tag{4.2}$$

and the value range for the ith bin will be

$$[r_{min} + i\Delta, r_{min} + (i+1)\Delta] \tag{4.3}$$
$$i = 0, 1, 2, \ldots N-1$$

The return values to use in calculations are the N values located at the center of each bin. These values are given by

$$r_i = r_{min} + \frac{(2i+1)\Delta}{2} \qquad (4.4)$$
$$i = 0, 1, 2, \ldots N-1$$

To find the associated probabilities, count the number of calculated returns that fall within the range of each bin. If the number in bin i is m_i and the total number of calculated returns is M, then the probability to associate with the ith return in eq.4.4 is

$$p_i = \frac{m_i}{M} \qquad i = 0, 1, 2, \ldots N-1 \qquad (4.5)$$

The usefulness or validity of this histogram approach is debatable. Past returns on a stock are not always reliable indicators of future returns. There is also the possibility of getting a return far outside the past range of returns. Stock market statistics change with time. In any event, the histogram can be used as a starting point. From there you can alter the returns and probabilities based on any additional information you may have that could influence the behavior of the stock price. You could also just base the returns and probabilities on your subjective belief of what the stock price will do. However you arrive at them, we will assume from here on that a stock has some finite set of possible returns r_i, $i = 0, 1, \ldots, N-1$ with associated probabilities p_i.

The analysis starts by assuming that you keep some fixed fraction f of your wealth or bankroll invested in the stock.

This means that at the end of each return period, you shift money into the stock if it had a negative return (the price went down) or out if it had a positive return in order to keep a constant fraction of your bankroll invested in the stock. The equation for the bankroll after n return periods is then

$$a_n = a_0 \prod_{k=0}^{n-1} (1 + r(k)f) \qquad (4.6)$$

where $r(k)$ is a random variable whose possible values are the returns r_i with probabilities p_i

$$P(r(k) = r_i) = p_i \qquad i = 0, 1, 2, \ldots N-1 \qquad (4.7)$$

Note that if there is only one possible return, r, with probability 1 then eq.4.6 becomes

$$a_n = a_0(1 + rf)^n \qquad (4.8)$$

This is the equation for a compound interest investment of a_0 at the interest rate rf. Clearly in this case you would want $f = 1$.

Now we want to apply the Kelly criterion which means finding the value of f that maximizes the expectation of $\log a_n$. That expectation is (assume $a_0 = 1$)

$$E[\log a_n] = \sum_{k=0}^{n-1} E[\log(1 + r(k)f] \qquad (4.9)$$

The expectation of the sum terms is

$$E[\log(1 + r(k)f] = \sum_{i=0}^{N-1} p_i \log(1 + r_i f) \qquad (4.10)$$

Substituting this into eq.4.9 gives

$$E[\log a_n] = n \sum_{i=0}^{N-1} p_i \log(1 + r_i f) = nG \qquad (4.11)$$

The summation is the long term exponential growth rate that we want to maximize. The maximum is found by setting the derivative of G with respect to f equal to zero and then solving for f. The equation is

$$\frac{dG}{df} = \sum_{i=0}^{N-1} \frac{p_i r_i}{1 + r_i f} = 0 \qquad (4.12)$$

This equation can generally only be solved numerically.

Below we will explain how to solve eq.4.12 numerically but first let's look at a simple example that can be solved by hand. Imagine a stock that has only two possible returns, a gain return, $r_0 = g$, that has probability p, and a loss return, $r_1 = -l$, that has probability $1 - p$. In this case eq.4.12 becomes

$$\frac{pg}{1 + gf} - \frac{(1 - p)l}{1 - lf} = 0 \qquad (4.13)$$

Solving this for f we get

$$f = \frac{pg - (1 - p)l}{gl} = \frac{(g + l)p - l}{gl} \qquad (4.14)$$

Substituting this back into the expression for G gives

$$G = \log(l + g) - p\log(l) - q\log(g) - H(p) \qquad (4.15)$$

where $H(p)$ is the binary entropy function (see eq.3.29).

Now let's look at the specific case of a stock that has an equal chance of doubling in value or decreasing to half its value in any given return period. This means $g = 1$, $l = \frac{1}{2}$, $p = \frac{1}{2}$ and the Kelly fraction is (using eq.4.14)

$$f = \frac{\frac{1}{2}(1) - \frac{1}{2}\left(\frac{1}{2}\right)}{(1)\left(\frac{1}{2}\right)} = \frac{1}{2}$$

To achieve long term exponential growth of your bankroll you should always keep $\frac{1}{2}$ of it invested in this stock. The exponential growth rate will be

$$G = \log\left(\frac{3}{2}\right) + \frac{1}{2}\log(2) - H(\frac{1}{2})$$
$$= 0.08496$$

using a base 2 logarithm.

Now let's look at how to solve the general problem given by eq.4.12.

Before trying to solve the problem directly let's look at what can be said about the possible values of f. First of all you can determine the sign of f by looking at the return expectation which is

$$E[r] = \sum_{i=0}^{N-1} p_i r_i \qquad (4.16)$$

If this expectation is negative, then f must be negative. You can never expect to gain by putting money in an investment with a negative expected return. The only way to make money on a stock with a negative expected return is to sell short the stock. This is what a negative f means, you sell short the stock instead of buying it. The value of f will be positive only if the expected return is positive. If the expected return is zero, then f will also be zero. You can see this by substituting $f = 0$ into eq.4.12 which then becomes

$$\sum_{i=0}^{N-1} p_i r_i = 0 \tag{4.17}$$

which states that the expected return is zero. The range of f can be further narrowed by noting that it appears in a logarithm in the equation for G (see eq.4.11). To keep G from becoming complex, the logarithm arguments must all be positive

$$1 + r_i f > 0 \qquad i = 0, 1, \ldots N-1 \tag{4.18}$$

Now if g is the most positive gain return, and $-l$ is the most negative loss return then eq.4.18 means that f must be restricted to the range

$$-\frac{1}{g} < f < \frac{1}{l} \tag{4.19}$$

We can then summarize the possible location of f as follows:

$$\text{If} \quad E[r] > 0 \qquad \text{then} \quad 0 < f < \frac{1}{l} \tag{4.20}$$

$$\text{If} \quad E[r] < 0 \qquad \text{then} \quad -\frac{1}{g} < f < 0$$

There will be only one unique value of f that solves eq.4.12 in either of these ranges. To see this, note that eq.4.12 is the logarithmic derivative of the function

$$\prod_{k=0}^{N-1} (1 + r_k f)^{p_k} \qquad (4.21)$$

This function is in factored form with N roots located at $f = -1/r_i$, $i = 0, 1, \ldots N - 1$. Clearly the maxima and minima of this function will be located in the intervals between the roots.

Now that the possible location of f has been narrowed down we can use a simple root finding algorithm to solve eq.4.12. Newton's root finding method will work very well for this problem. The method is easy to describe geometrically. To find the root of a function $F(x)$ you start with an initial guess x_0. The next guess x_1 is taken as the intercept of the tangent line at x_0 with the x-axis. The slope of the tangent line is $F'(x_0)$ so that we have

$$F'(x_0) = \frac{F(x_0)}{x_0 - x_1} \qquad (4.22)$$

Solving this for x_1 gives

$$x_1 = x_0 - \frac{F(x_0}{F'(x_0)} \qquad (4.23)$$

The next guess x_2 is found similarly from x_1 and so on as expressed in the recursion equation

$$x_{i+1} = x_i - \frac{F(x_i)}{F'(x_i)} \qquad (4.24)$$

The process is continued until the difference

$$\Delta = x_{i+1} - x_i < \epsilon \tag{4.25}$$

where ϵ is some number close to zero, i.e. $\epsilon = 0.00001$ is a good choice for this problem.

At this point $F(x_i) \approx 0$. Newton's method can sometimes produce errors when the tangent line intercepts start moving away from the desired root but this is not a problem in this case since we know the interval that the root is located in and can correct for this possibility.

Now let's apply the method to solving eq.4.12. First note that when the terms in the sum are combined then the function that we want to find the root of is the numerator of the combined sum. This function can be expressed as

$$
\begin{aligned}
h(f) &= \prod_{j=0}^{N-1}(1 + r_j f) \sum_{i=0}^{N-1} \frac{p_i r_i}{1 + r_i f} \tag{4.26} \\
&= \sum_{i=0}^{N-1} p_i r_i \prod_{j \neq i}(1 + r_j f)
\end{aligned}
$$

Finding the root then involves iterating

$$f_{i+1} = f_i - \frac{h(f_i)}{h'(f_i)} \tag{4.27}$$

The initial guess can be taken as the midpoint of the interval determined by the rules in eq.4.20. Taking the derivatives, eq.4.27 can be reduced to the following form

$$f_{i+1} = f_i - \frac{1}{s_1 - \frac{s_3}{s_2}} \tag{4.28}$$

where

$$s_1 = \sum_{k=0}^{N-1} r_k(1 + r_k f_i)^{-1} \tag{4.29}$$

$$s_2 = \sum_{k=0}^{N-1} p_k r_k(1 + r_k f_i)^{-1} \tag{4.30}$$

$$s_3 = \sum_{k=0}^{N-1} p_k r_k^2(1 + r_k f_i)^{-2} \tag{4.31}$$

A solution to the problem of potentially having $1 + r_k f_i = 0$ in the above equations is to just set $1 + r_k f_i = 0.00001$ when this happens. Python code for implementing this algorithm is shown below. The function that performs the calculation is called frac_single. The function takes two arguments. The first argument is a list containing the return probabilities and the second argument is the list of returns. There is no limit on the number of returns that can be used. The value returned by the function is the Kelly fraction.

```
class single_iter(object):
  def __init__(self, prbv, retv):
    self.prbv = prbv
    self.retv = retv
  def f(self, x):
    s1 = s2 = s3 = d1 = d2 = d3 = 0
    for k in range(len(self.prbv)):
      pk = self.prbv[k]
      rk = self.retv[k]
      d1 = 1 + rk * x
      if d1 == 0: d1 = 0.000001
      d2 = rk / d1
      d3 = pk * d2
      s1 += d2
      s2 += d3
      s3 += d2 * d3
    return x - s2 / ( s1 * s2 - s3)

def expectation(prbv, retv):
  e = 0
  for i in range(len(prbv)):
    e += prbv[i] * retv[i]
  return e

def frac_single(prbv, retv):
  fiter = single_iter(prbv, retv)
  gmax = max(retv)
  lmax = min(retv)

  xmin = xmax = 0
  if expectation(prbv, retv) >= 0:
    if lmax >= 0:
      return 1  # this should be +inf
    else:
      xmax = -1 / lmax
  else:
    if gmax <= 0:
      return -1  # this should be -inf
    else:
```

```
    xmin = -1 / gmax

xstart = (xmin + xmax) / 2
x0 = xstart
x1 = fiter.f(xstart)
while abs(x1 - x0) > 0.00001:
   if x1 > xmax: x1 = xmax
   if x1 < xmin: x1 = xmin
   x0 = x1
   x1 = fiter.f(x1)
return x1
```

4.2   Single Stock and Risk Free Bond

The single stock analysis in the previous section changes somewhat if we include the possibility of a risk free investment. This is an investment with a guaranteed rate of return which we will call r_f. In practice the closest you can get to a risk free investment is a Treasury security. We will call this type of investment a risk free bond.

Let f_1 be the fraction invested in the stock, and f_2 the fraction invested in the bond. Then the bankroll equation becomes

$$a_n = a_0 \prod_{k=0}^{n-1} (1 + r(k)f_1 + r_f f_2) \qquad (4.32)$$

Now assume that whatever is not invested in the stock is invested in the bond. In that case $f_1 + f_2 = 1$ and eq.4.32

can be written as (from here on assume $a_0 = 1$)

$$a_n = \prod_{k=0}^{n-1} (1 + r_f + (r(k) - r_f)f_1) \tag{4.33}$$

The expectation of $\log a_n$ is

$$\begin{aligned}
E[\log a_n] &= \sum_{k=0}^{n-1} E[\log(1 + r_f + (r(k) - r_f)f_1)] \tag{4.34} \\
&= nG
\end{aligned}$$

$$\begin{aligned}
G &= E[\log(1 + r_f + (r(k) - r_f)f_1)] \tag{4.35} \\
&= \sum_{i=0}^{N-1} p_i \log(1 + r_f + (r_i - r_f)f_1)
\end{aligned}$$

This is the exponential growth rate that we want to maximize. As before we want to solve

$$\frac{dG}{df_1} = \sum_{i=0}^{N-1} \frac{p_i(r_i - r_f)}{1 + r_f + (r_i - r_f)f_1} = 0 \tag{4.36}$$

Analogous to eq.4.18 for the stock only investment, the following condition must be satisfied

$$1 + r_f + (r_i - r_f)f_1 > 0 \qquad i = 0, 1, \ldots N-1 \qquad (4.37)$$

If g is the most positive gain return and $-l$ is the most negative loss return, then this condition means that f_1 must be in the interval

$$-\frac{1+r_f}{g - r_f} < f_1 < \frac{1+r_f}{l + r_f} \qquad (4.38)$$

The rules in eq.4.20 become

$$\text{If} \quad E[r] > r_f \qquad \text{then} \quad 0 < f_1 < \frac{1+r_f}{l+r_f} \qquad (4.39)$$

$$\text{If} \quad E[r] < r_f \qquad \text{then} \quad -\frac{1+r_f}{g-r_f} < f_1 < 0$$

Note that it is easy to see that if $E[r] = r_f$, i.e. the expected return on the stock is equal to the risk free return, then $f_1 = 0$. In this case you should invest nothing in the stock and put all your money in the risk free bond.

It is straightforward to adapt the algorithm for calculating the single stock fraction to calculating the fraction in this case. We leave it to the reader to do this.

When the stock has only two possible returns, a gain g and a loss $-l$ then the stock fraction can be solved for exactly. The result is

$$f_1 = (1 + r_f) \left[\frac{r_f - pg + ql}{(r_f - g)(r_f + l)} \right] \qquad (4.40)$$

where p is the gain probability and $q = 1 - p$ is the loss probability. You can see clearly here that $f_1 = 0$ when

$$r_f = pg - ql \qquad (4.41)$$

In other words don't invest in the stock if the expected return is just equal to the risk free interest rate.

You can also use eq.4.40 to analyze an investment in a risky bond. A risky bond is like a stock with $g = r$ being the interest rate and $l = 1$ being the loss when the bond defaults. Substituting these values into eq.4.40 gives you the fraction that should be invested in the risky bond

$$\begin{aligned} f &= (1 + r_f) \frac{(r_f - pr + q)}{(r_f - r)(r_f + 1)} \qquad (4.42) \\ &= 1 + q \left(\frac{r + 1}{r_f - r} \right) \end{aligned}$$

where q in this case is the probability that the bond defaults. Now from eq.4.42 you can determine the limit on the default probability that would still allow investment in the bond, i.e. make $f \geq 0$. The limit is

$$q \leq \frac{r - r_f}{r + 1} \qquad (4.43)$$

If the default probability obeys this condition then you should invest in the bond.

Of course it is not possible to know the default probability with any certainty but you can use eq.4.43 to calculate the maximum default probability, q_{max}

$$q_{max} = \frac{r - r_f}{r + 1} \qquad (4.44)$$

given the current market interest rate for the bond, r, and the risk free rate r_f. You are then essentially allowing the market to determine the default probability for you.

4.3   Two Stock Investment

In this final section we will look at investing in two stocks simultaneously. Let x and y be the bankroll fractions invested in the two stocks, then the bankroll equation is

$$a_n = a_0 \prod_{k=0}^{n-1} (1 + r(k)x + s(k)y) \qquad (4.45)$$

where $r(k)$ and $s(k)$ are random variables representing the returns on the stocks. Let M and N be the number of possible returns for $r(k)$ and $s(k)$, and denote those values as

$$r(k) = r_i \quad , \quad i = 0, 1, \ldots, M-1 \tag{4.46}$$
$$s(k) = s_j \quad , \quad j = 0, 1, \ldots, N-1$$

In general the returns may be correlated in which case the joint probability distribution is

$$P(r(k) = r_i, s(k) = s_j) = p_{ij} \tag{4.47}$$

If the returns are independent, then the joint distribution factors into a product

$$
\begin{aligned}
P(r(k) = r_i, s(k) = s_j) &= P(r(k) = r_i)P(s(k) = s_j) \\
&= p_i q_j \tag{4.48}
\end{aligned}
$$

where the p_i are the probabilities associated with $r(k)$ and the q_j are associated with $s(k)$.

Now we want to find the fractions x and y that maximize the expectation of $\log a_n$ which is (assume $a_0 = 1$)

$$
\begin{aligned}
E[\log(a_n)] &= \sum_{k=0}^{n-1} E[\log(1 + r(k)x + s(k)y)] \\
&= nG \tag{4.49}
\end{aligned}
$$

G is the exponential growth rate that needs to be maximized.

$$G = E[\log(1 + r(k)x + s(k)y)] \qquad (4.50)$$

$$= \sum_{i=0}^{M-1} \sum_{j=0}^{N-1} p_{ij} \log(1 + r_i x + s_j y)$$

Finding the maximum of this with respect to x and y involves solving the following two equations

$$\frac{\partial G}{\partial x} = \sum_{i=0}^{M-1} \sum_{j=0}^{N-1} \frac{p_{ij} r_i}{1 + r_i x + s_j y} = 0 \qquad (4.51)$$

$$\frac{\partial G}{\partial y} = \sum_{i=0}^{M-1} \sum_{j=0}^{N-1} \frac{p_{ij} s_j}{1 + r_i x + s_j y} = 0$$

First we can narrow down the possible values of x and y by noting that the arguments of the log functions in eq.4.50 must be positive. This means that for all i and j the following condition must hold

$$1 + r_i x + s_j y > 0 \qquad (4.52)$$

Now if r_0 and s_0 are the most positive gain returns and r_{M-1} and s_{N-1} are the most negative loss returns on the stocks, then eq.4.52 will hold if the following two conditions are met.

$$-\frac{1}{r_0} < x < -\frac{1}{r_{M-1}} \tag{4.53}$$

$$-\frac{1}{s_0} < y < -\frac{1}{s_{N-1}}$$

This confines the possible solutions to the regions labeled 1, 2, 3, and 4 in fig.4.1.

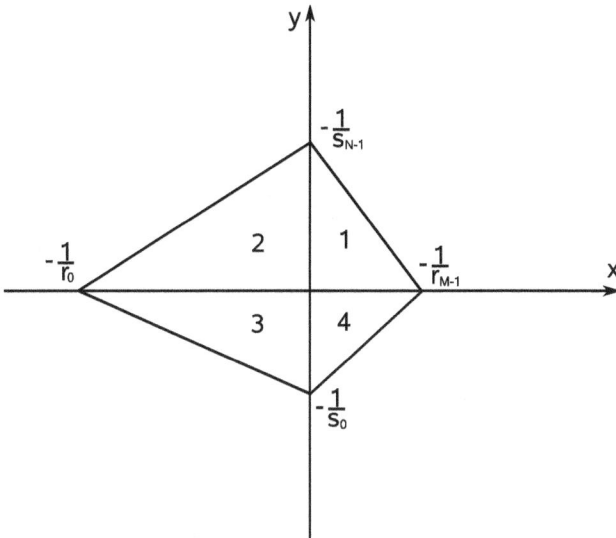

Figure 4.1: Solution regions for returns on two simultaneous stock investments.

The solution can further be narrowed down by noting that if the expected value of $r(k)$ is positive/negative, then x will be positive/negative and likewise for $s(k)$ and y. Those expected values are

$$E[r] = \sum_{i=0}^{M-1} p_i r_i \qquad (4.54)$$

$$E[s] = \sum_{j=0}^{N-1} q_j s_j$$

where p_i and q_j are in general related to the joint distribution as follows

$$p_i = \sum_{j=0}^{N-1} p_{ij} \qquad (4.55)$$

$$q_j = \sum_{i=0}^{M-1} p_{ij}$$

The solution region is then narrowed down as follows

If $E[r] > 0$ and $E[s] > 0$ then solution is in region 1
If $E[r] < 0$ and $E[s] > 0$ then solution is in region 2
If $E[r] < 0$ and $E[s] < 0$ then solution is in region 3
If $E[r] > 0$ and $E[s] < 0$ then solution is in region 4

Now to solve eq.4.51 we will use a two dimensional Newton root finding algorithm. Let $f(x, y)$ and $g(x, y)$ be the two functions that we want to find the root of, i.e. we want to solve the simultaneous equations

$$
\begin{aligned}
f(x, y) &= 0 \\
g(x, y) &= 0
\end{aligned}
\tag{4.56}
$$

The Newton's method for solving these equations can simply be stated as follows. Start at some initial point (x, y) in the neighborhood of the root and find increments Δx and Δy that solve the equations

$$
\begin{aligned}
f(x, y) + \frac{\partial f}{\partial x} \Delta x + \frac{\partial f}{\partial y} \Delta y &= 0 \\
g(x, y) + \frac{\partial g}{\partial x} \Delta x + \frac{\partial g}{\partial y} \Delta y &= 0
\end{aligned}
\tag{4.57}
$$

Next update the initial point $(x, y) \rightarrow (x + \Delta x, y + \Delta y)$ and repeat the process. Continue this until Δx and Δy approach zero to within some tolerance level. At this point you will have an approximate solution of eqs.4.56.

The solutions of eqs.4.57 for Δx and Δy is

$$
\begin{aligned}
\Delta x &= \frac{g \frac{\partial f}{\partial y} - f \frac{\partial g}{\partial y}}{D} \\
\Delta y &= \frac{f \frac{\partial g}{\partial x} - g \frac{\partial f}{\partial x}}{D}
\end{aligned}
\tag{4.58}
$$

where

$$D = \frac{\partial f}{\partial x}\frac{\partial g}{\partial y} - \frac{\partial f}{\partial y}\frac{\partial g}{\partial x} \qquad (4.59)$$

The functions that we want to find the root of are the numerators of the combined sums in eq.4.51. Therefore let

$$f(x,y) = P \sum_{i=0}^{M-1} \sum_{j=0}^{N-1} \frac{p_{ij} r_i}{1 + r_i x + s_j y} \qquad (4.60)$$

$$g(x,y) = P \sum_{i=0}^{M-1} \sum_{j=0}^{N-1} \frac{p_{ij} s_j}{1 + r_i x + s_j y}$$

where

$$P = \prod_{i=0}^{M-1} \prod_{j=0}^{N-1} (1 + r_i x + s_j y) \qquad (4.61)$$

The derivatives of $f(x,y)$ and $g(x,y)$ are then

$$\frac{\partial f}{\partial x} = \left(\sum R_{ij} \sum p_{ij} R_{ij} - \sum p_{ij} R_{ij}^2 \right) P \quad (4.62)$$

$$\frac{\partial f}{\partial y} = \left(\sum S_{ij} \sum p_{ij} R_{ij} - \sum p_{ij} R_{ij} S_{ij} \right) P$$

$$\frac{\partial g}{\partial x} = \left(\sum R_{ij} \sum p_{ij} S_{ij} - \sum p_{ij} R_{ij} S_{ij} \right) P$$

$$\frac{\partial g}{\partial y} = \left(\sum S_{ij} \sum p_{ij} S_{ij} - \sum p_{ij} S_{ij}^2 \right) P$$

where

$$\sum = \sum_{i=0}^{M-1} \sum_{j=0}^{N-1} \quad (4.63)$$

$$R_{ij} = r_i (1 + r_i x + s_j y)^{-1}$$

$$S_{ij} = s_j (1 + r_i x + s_j y)^{-1}$$

Substituting these expressions into eq.4.58 for Δx and Δy will cause the P factors to cancel out. This means that they do not have to be included in the calculations. They still need to be included in the definition of $f(x,y)$ and $g(x,y)$ however, since the derivative will have a different form without them, and if you use that form then the convergence of the algorithm will be slower. Listed below is Python code that calculates the fractions x and y using the above algorithm for two stocks with any number of returns. The returns are specified in the two lists **ret1v** and **ret2v** with the corresponding probabilities in the lists

prb1v and **prb2v**. If the returns are not independent then
the marginal distributions in eq.4.55 should be used for the
probabilities. Note also that the code listed below uses the
code for the single stock calculation.

```
class double_iter(object):
  def __init__(self, prb1v, ret1v, prb2v, ret2v):
    self.prb1v = prb1v
    self.ret1v = ret1v
    self.prb2v = prb2v
    self.ret2v = ret2v
  def f(self, v0):
    x = v0[0]
    y = v0[1]
    s1 = s2 = s3 = s4 = s5 = s6 = s7 = d1 = 0
    Rkl = Skl = pklRkl = pklSkl = 0
    for k in range(len(self.prb1v)):
      pk = self.prb1v[k]
      rk = self.ret1v[k]
      for l in range(len(self.prb2v)):
        pl = self.prb2v[l]
        sl = self.ret2v[l]
        d1 = 1 + rk * x + sl * y
        if d1 == 0: d1 = 0.000001
        Rkl = rk / d1
        Skl = sl / d1
        pklRkl = pk * pl * Rkl
        pklSkl = pk * pl * Skl
        s1 += Rkl
        s2 += Skl
        s3 += pklRkl
        s4 += pklSkl
        s5 += pklRkl * Rkl
        s6 += pklSkl * Skl
        s7 += pklRkl * Skl
    fx = s1 * s3 - s5
    fy = s2 * s3 - s7
    gx = s1 * s4 - s7
```

```
  gy = s2 * s4 - s6
  det = fx * gy - fy * gx
  dx = (s4 * fy - s3 * gy) / det
  dy = (s3 * gx - s4 * fx) / det
  return [x + dx, y + dy]

def frac_double(prb1v, ret1v, prb2v, ret2v):
  fiter = double_iter(prb1v, ret1v, prb2v, ret2v)
  xstart = frac_single(prb1v, ret1v)
  ystart = frac_single(prb2v, ret2v)
  vstart = [xstart, ystart]

  if xstart >= 0:
    xmin = 0
    xmax = xstart
  else:
    xmin = xstart
    xmax = 0

  if ystart >= 0:
    ymin = 0
    ymax = ystart
  else:
    ymin = ystart
    ymax = 0

  if abs(xstart) == 1 or abs(ystart) == 1: return vstart
  v0 = vstart
  v1 = fiter.f(vstart)
  while abs(v1[0]-v0[0]) > 0.00001 or abs(v1[1]-v0[1]) > 0.00001:
    if v1[0] > xmax: v1[0] = xmax
    if v1[0] < xmin: v1[0] = xmin
    if v1[1] > ymax: v1[1] = ymax
    if v1[1] < ymin: v1[1] = ymin
    v0 = v1
    v1 = fiter.f(v1)
  return v1
```

Bibliography

[1] L. Breiman. Optimal gambling systems for favorable games. *Proceedings of the Fourth Berkeley Symposium on Mathematical Statistics and Probability*, I:65–78, 1961.

[2] Lester E. Dubins and Leonard J. Savage. *How to gamble if you must; inequalities for stochastic processes.* McGraw-Hill series in probability and statistics. McGraw-Hill, 1965.

[3] Richard A. Epstein. *The theory of gambling and statistical logic.* Academic Press, 1977.

[4] S.N. Ethier. The kelly system maximizes median fortune. *Journal of Applied Probability*, 41(4):1230–1236, dec 2004.

[5] S.N. Ethier and S. Tavar. The proportional bettor's return on investment. *Journal of Applied Probability*, 20(3):563–573, sept 1983.

[6] William Feller. *An introduction to probability theory and its applications.* Wiley, 1957.

[7] J.L. Kelly. A new interpretation of information rate. *The Bell System Technical Journal*, 35:917–926, july 1956.

[8] Edward W. Packel. *The mathematics of games and gambling*. Anneli Lax new mathematical library, 28. Mathematical Association of America, 2006.

[9] William Poundstone. *Fortune's Formula: The Untold Story of the Scientific Betting System that Beat the Casinos and Wall Street*. Hill and Wang, 2005.

[10] David G. Schwartz. *Roll the bones : the history of gambling*. Gotham Books, 2006.

[11] E.O. Thorp. Optimal gambling systems for favorable games. *Review of the International Statistical Institute*, 37(3):273–293, 1969.

[12] E.O. Thorp. *The Mathematics of Gambling*. Gambling Times, 1985.

[13] E.O. Thorp. The kelly criterion in blackjack sports betting, and the stock market. *Handbook of Asset and Liability Management, Volume 1*, 2006.

[14] Olaf Vancura, Judy A. Cornelius, and William R. Eadington. *Finding the edge : mathematical analysis of casino games*. Institute for the Study of Gambling and Commercial Gaming, 2000.

[15] Stanford Wong. What proportional betting does to your win rate. *Blackjack World,*, 3:162–168, 1981.

Index

average, 9

Bell System Technical Journal, 57
Bernoulli approach, 53, 59
Bernoulli, Daniel, 56
Bernoulli-Kelly system, 59
binomial coefficient, 21, 95
binomial expansion, 31, 52

cancellation betting, 45
coin toss, 7, 20, 21, 56
communication channel, 57–59
communication theory, 58
continuous function, 53
covariance, 16

default probability, 101, 117, 118
dice, 7, 11, 58

entropy function, 59
  binary, 61, 80, 82, 107

expectation, 10, 12, 13, 15, 28, 34, 35, 37, 41, 45, 50–56, 58–60, 65, 73, 74, 76, 84, 87, 89, 90, 98, 99, 105, 108, 115, 119
  linearity property, 13
exponential growth rate factor, 57, 59, 60, 84, 90, 106, 115, 119

fixed fraction betting, 49, 52, 60

gambling systems, 28
games
  N identical, 86
  dependent, 76
  independent, 74, 76
  single, 83, 90
  three simultaneous, 84
  two simultaneous, 72
general gambling equation, 28, 49

About the Authors

Stefan Hollos and **Richard Hollos** are physicists by training, and now work in quantitative finance. They are brothers, and business partners at QuantWolf where they develop quantitative finance software. Their interests include risk management, pricing financial derivatives, statistical arbitrage, algorithmic trading, and financial market modeling. They are available for consulting.

You can contact them at their workplace website
`http://quantwolf.com/`

www.ingramcontent.com/pod-product-compliance
Lightning Source LLC
Chambersburg PA
CBHW021105210326
41598CB00016B/1331